MW00487434

White Poverty

BOOKS BY REVEREND DR. WILLIAM BARBER II

We Are Called to Be a Movement

Revive Us Again:
Vision and Action in Moral Organizing

The Third Reconstruction:
How a Moral Movement Is Overcoming
the Politics of Division and Fear

BOOKS BY REVEREND DR. WILLIAM BARBER II AND
PROFESSOR JONATHAN WILSON-HARTGROVE

The Third Reconstruction:
The Story of Moral Mondays, Fusion Politics,
and the Rise of a New Justice Movement

White Poverty

How Exposing Myths About Race and Class Can Reconstruct American Democracy

Reverend Dr. William J. Barber II

with Jonathan Wilson-Hartgrove

Liveright Publishing Corporation

A Division of W. W. Norton & Company
Independent Publishers Since 1923

PHOTO ON THE PREVIOUS SPREAD:
*A group of 25,000 people gathered at the National Mall
for the Poor People's Campaign, 2018.*

—

Copyright © 2024 by Reverend Dr. William J. Barber

All rights reserved
Printed in the United States of America
First Edition

For information about permission to reproduce selections from this
book, write to Permissions, Liveright Publishing Corporation, a
division of W. W. Norton & Company, Inc., 500 Fifth Avenue,
New York, NY 10110

For information about special discounts for bulk purchases, please
contact W. W. Norton Special Sales at specialsales@wwnorton.com
or 800-233-4830

Manufacturing by Lakeside Book Company
Book design by Lovedog Studio
Production manager: Lauren Abbate

ISBN 978-1-324-09487-6

Liveright Publishing Corporation, 500 Fifth Avenue,
New York, N.Y. 10110
www.wwnorton.com

W. W. Norton & Company Ltd., 15 Carlisle Street,
London W1D 3BS

1 2 3 4 5 6 7 8 9 0

Contents

PREFACE

THIS IS A BOOK BY A BLACK MAN ABOUT WHITE poverty in America. I've written *White Poverty* because I believe the racist images of Black mothers on welfare that have dominated the imaginations of Americans are not merely demeaning to Black people; they are also based on a myth that obscures the poverty of tens of millions of white people. Until we face the reality of white poverty in America, we cannot comprehend what is truly exceptional about the inequality that persists in the richest nation in the history of the world.

I've written this book to ask America to look its poor—*all* its poor—in the face and acknowledge that those faces are overwhelmingly white.

We rarely face this basic fact because of America's oldest myths. Humans do not have the capacity to see everything the eye beholds, so we develop ways to focus our attention. Myths are the shared stories that tell us what to see. When natural dangers lurked at the edge of ancient villages, people told stories of monsters in the forest to focus their attention on potential threats. When seafaring people sent boats out to sea that never came home, they developed myths about creatures that lurked in the deep, able to consume whole crews along with their cargo. Humans have used myths to survive, helping their children pay attention to threats they might otherwise overlook. Myths then train us to see, but they also blind us. To face the realities we've been taught to ignore, we must shed so many of the myths that have dominated our past.

"Not everything that is faced can be changed," James Baldwin once observed, "but nothing can be changed until it is faced." I want America to face white poverty because I know that change is possible, and I maintain this hope despite evidence to the contrary because I know who I am.

I was born two days *after* the March on Washington on August 28, 1963. My mother has always said she went into labor during the march, but I waited around for two days to see how things were going to turn out. A quarter million people—*Black and white together*—filled the National Mall to dramatize the fact that a mass movement was rising to demand change. As Martin Luther King Jr. said in his speech that day, America's promise of equality had come back like a bounced check in the images of Black children rolled across pavement with fire hoses and attacked by police dogs for marching peacefully to protest second-class citizenship. A young John Lewis made clear in his speech that this movement wasn't demanding only civil rights, but also economic justice for those "receiving starvation wages, or no wages at all."

At a hospital in Indianapolis, Indiana, two days later, my father objected to the designation of "Negro" on my birth certificate, as if to suggest that I was but a compartmentalized human being. He was hardly ashamed of being Black. My father and mother were both active in the Civil Rights movement and came from a tradition that taught us to be proud of

Black people and all we have contributed to America and to the world.

My father insisted that I never deny any part of who I am. Yes, I am Black. But that's not all that I am. Our family descends from Tuscaroran Indians, free Black people, and people of European descent with eyes as blue as the Atlantic Ocean that brought our settler and enslaved ancestors together to this land. My father would not let the government say that I was simply a "Negro." He knew the blood lines that connect so many of us in America already formed a three-fold chord in my DNA. We are not a binary nation, efficiently divided into Black and white.

Yet I am convinced that we as a nation have forgotten who we are. Since the emergence of the Tea Party following the election of President Barack Obama and the reactionary rise of Donald Trump and the MAGA movement in Republican Party politics, it has become a truism of political pundits that we are a nation more divided than ever. In a sense, of course, this is true. I am not blind to reality. The lies of the old myths that have been used to divide Americans throughout our history are now amplified—the volume turned up not only by political campaigns, but also by the wrap-around cycle of cable news, by the culture of social media, by corporation-funded and billionaire-subsidized activists, and by officious school board members determined to stamp out "political correctness."

Yet while these same fights are regularly recycled for our public consumption, nearly half of Americans—people of every race, creed, and region—are united by the experience of being poor. They share the hardship, but they do not share a name because our formal definition of poverty has left tens of millions of Americans in the shadows. Even when we hear reports about poverty, they are based on numbers that severely under-count Americans who are living with their backs against the wall, unsure how they are going to make it.

We must redefine poverty, as I will argue, in order to cap-ture the crisis people are facing. The numbers and language we currently use to name poverty in America are a lie. In fact, they constitute a *damn* lie. One of the most damnable features of our common life is the way we talk about poverty as if it's an anomaly and not a feature of our economic system.

Despite consistent gains over decades in the Gross Domestic Product (GDP) and stock market indices, real wealth for most Americans has steadily declined over the past half century. In 2016 there was *not a single county* in the United States where someone working full time at minimum wage could afford to rent a simple two-bedroom apartment. That's poverty, and it's past time we demand that our government expand its definition to recognize this fact.

When I talk about poverty in this book, I'm talking about every American who lives on the edge—not because they choose to, but because of policy decisions we continue to make as a nation. It's critical to name that poverty isn't an isolated experience in America. *It is everywhere.* And while it dispro-portionately weighs on Black and brown people, this basic fact of American inequality remains hidden in plain sight: white people are by far the largest racial demographic among America's poor.

White poverty isn't just the woman asking for spare change at the top of the exit ramp or the man sleeping in Penn Station. It's the mother who bags your groceries in the check-out line but doesn't know how she's going to feed her kids if she pays to fix the car that's her only ride back to work tomorrow. It's the college graduate who has a job but doesn't earn enough each month to rent his own place and pay back his student loans. It is the construction day laborer without health insurance for him and his family. It's the warehouse worker in a so-called "right to work" state who is forced to choose between buying her medicine or paying her rent. It's tens of millions of Americans who live and work in almost every community, though they often have to sleep in their car or take a shower at a friend's house.

From attention to the opioid crisis to reporting on "deaths of despair" in rural communities, we experience occasional glimpses of how poverty impacts white Americans. But whenever we focus for a moment on the connections between drug use in inner cities and Appalachia or the impact of poverty on Native American children in Arizona and poor white children in West Virginia or Indiana or upstate New York, it seems we are inevitably interrupted by another story suggesting that poor people are to blame for their situation. Even if their skin is white, poor folks are accused of sinking into the so-called "culture of poverty" that traps Black, brown, and Native communities. Poverty, this myth insists, is the fault of those who are poor.

But the myths that blame Black people for their poverty and call white people "trash" when they experience the same begin to unravel when we face the reality that there are more than twice as many poor white people as there are poor Black people in this nation. Politicians sometimes call poor white folks "working class" or "those aspiring to the middle class," but when we count them with all other poor Americans, we can see that poverty is the canker consuming our common life. Yes, racism persists, making rates of poverty higher in communities of color. But the same lie that blames Black people for their poverty also prevents us from seeing the pain of poor families who have been offered little more than "whiteness" and angry tweets to sustain them in an economy where the cost of housing, healthcare, education, and transportation have skyrocketed while wages have stagnated for almost all Americans.

Here's what I know about poverty in America: it's an experience that isolates millions of white people. But apart from the myths that tell them to be ashamed and silent about what they're going through, it has the potential to unite them with one another and millions of neighbors who clean office buildings and work in public schools, pick produce and put it on grocery store shelves, package mail orders and deliver them to our homes, take care of children while their parents work, and clean and feed aging parents whose adult children are at the office. At a moment when so much public attention is focused on division, the shared experience of poverty has the potential to unite a movement for genuine change, which is what this book is about.

Maps that show "red" counties and "blue" counties in the United States represent election results that have implications for our government's capacity to pass legislation that could address poverty. But these maps only represent the majority of the people whose votes are counted in any given election. Places that are controlled by reactionary extremists who serve corporate interests are not "red" counties so much as they are unorganized counties where the largest bloc of voters isn't Republican or Democrat, but rather poor people who often do not vote. These people haven't opted out of the political process because they don't recognize something is amiss. The problem is that no one is offering to represent them, and they have work to do—whether they be nurses, factory workers, waitresses, or house painters—to try to make ends meet on the first Tuesday in November.

Still, those maps of "red" and "blue" counties tell a story that many Americans have come to believe. They are a myth in the truest sense—a story told to us in order to reinforce the values of the storytellers. We need a better story about who we are and who we want to be. I've written *White Poverty* from my own experience as a Black civil rights and moral leader who has been invited into struggles across America led by poor white people. But I have not written it alone. Twenty-five years ago, when I was a much younger preacher and community activist, I met Jonathan Wilson-Hartgrove, a young white man from the hills of North Carolina. Our friendship has been a personal experience of the "moral fusion"—a term you'll hear more about later—that promises the possibility of a multiethnic democracy where all of us can thrive. I've asked him to tell more of his story in his own voice in the epilogue of this book.

In the summer of 2020, after the public murder of George Floyd by Minneapolis police, America experienced one of the largest mass demonstrations for racial justice in our nation's history. We watched people of every race marching together in big cities and in small towns, determined to transform the systems of white supremacy that have crushed Black lives. In response to this uprising, we have also witnessed a backlash of resentment that has demonized anti-racism, banned books, and sown division among people who overwhelmingly affirmed the basic assertion that "Black Lives Matter."

I realize that, in this moment, it may seem strange that a Black man who stands in the long tradition of Black-led freedom struggle would write a book about *white* poverty. Some of my friends worry that if a Black person lifts the lid that obscures white poverty, it somehow diminishes the urgency of addressing Black people's pain. But I contend that it actually intensifies the urgency—and in a good way. I take on white poverty as a declaration that Black people may have problems, but we are *not* the problem. Other people face the same struggles we do. It doesn't make any sense to try to fight this battle on our own. It's past time that we come together and stop being played against one another. We need to link up with anyone who can see that we're living in a society where it's hard for most of us to get by, while an increasingly smaller number of people at the top enjoy an unimaginable amount of wealth.

White folks, I fully realize, have their own reasons to be suspicious of someone who capitalizes "Black" but writes "white" in lowercase. Who is to say that a Black man writing about white poverty doesn't just want to see the tables turned, with Black people up on top? Throughout this book, I explain why I believe all of us need to rethink who our people really are. Race in America gave us a constellation of myths that are designed to divide us. Many white people belong to families and places, folkways and communities that give them rich identities. I've met Appalachian folk and Okies, Acadians and Midwestern farmers who share a strong sense of who they are. But those identities—all capitalized—are much thicker than whiteness. The truth is, "whiteness" is a false identity designed to unite people who don't actually share much in common behind an economic and political system that doesn't serve most of us.

I capitalize "Black" and "Native" because they name shared cultures that developed practices of resistance against these myths. Many groups of white folks have also developed their own cultures of resistance. *Craqueros* in colonial Florida were cattle drivers of British descent who were looked down on by Spanish landowners. Like oppressed people throughout the history of the world, some of them embraced a term intended as an insult and became proud Crackers. Likewise with Rednecks in Appalachia. They took their name from a derogatory term for poor white field workers whose necks were regularly sunburned and donned red bandanas as a sign of solidarity in their struggle against the mining companies. Most folks don't remember when they talk about Rednecks today that, while most of those miners were white, some were Black, too. My grandfather on my mother's side—a holiness preacher—was a Black miner in West Virginia back in the days of the Coal Wars, when Black and white miners were attacked for trying to form a union in the Battle of Blair Mountain.

When I pause to reflect on the lessons that my ancestors have passed down to me, I know there's not a message that's more important for this moment than the call to face white poverty and embrace an identity that unites poor and working people of every race. The fundamental structure of inequality in America remains shrouded in the myths that plantation owners told poor European immigrants to make them believe that laws which allowed planters to own human beings would ultimately serve the interests of those poor white immigrants. While there have been, in every generation of this nation's history, Horatio Alger stories that kept this myth alive, white poverty remains as the troubling fact that exposes the lie.

I've written *White Poverty* then because I know that the truth can set us free. When we face the fact of America's unique inequality, we encounter the people who have the power to change it. Nothing can be changed until it is faced, it's true. I've written this book because I've faced white poverty and met the people who can help us become the nation we have never yet been.

I want you to know them, too.

William J. Barber II
New Haven, Connecticut
September 2023

PART I

Facing Poverty

*Rev. Barber discussing poverty with community
members in Aberdeen, Washington.*

Chapter 1

THE CRISIS
WE CANNOT SEE

I WAS SITTING IN THE STUDY OF THE CHURCH I PAS-
tored for thirty years when one of our deacons knocked on
the door. "Pastor, do you have a minute?"

"Come on in," I said.

"We've got a young woman here asking if we can help her
with fifty dollars to pay her light bill," the deacon said.

In the New Testament, which tells the story of the beginning of the church, deacons were assigned to serve the early
Christian community by making sure that the most vulnerable
among us have what they need. This retired Black man in a
military town in eastern North Carolina was doing a job passed
down to him by millennia of church tradition. He was helping
our community respond to the people whom the Scriptures call
"widows and orphans."

"Who is it?" I asked, and he told me her name.

"Let's do it," I replied, moving quickly to try to figure out
how we could get the money to the power company before they
sent someone out to shut off her electricity. I'd already been pas-
toring long enough to know that folks in the community almost
never come to ask for help until there's little to no time left.

"But pastor," this deacon interrupted, "do you think we

also need to do something to help her find a job?" He couldn't imagine that a working person could be in a situation where she wasn't able to pay her bills, but I knew this woman. She worked two jobs and still barely made enough to keep a roof over her head. An unexpected flat tire on her old hand-me-down car was an emergency. A new set of four tires was an unimaginable expense.

This deacon was a good man with a good heart, but I realized that day in my study that he couldn't see the poor people that the church had asked him to serve. This wasn't a personal failure on his part. It was, instead, a result of the shared myths that shape how most Americans think about poverty. As a pastor, I recognized that our church could not do the job we were called to do without learning to see the people who were hidden from us by forces we did not understand.

What was true for our community is also true for America: we are, as a people, unable to address the crisis of poverty because we do not see it. The older I get, the more I'm troubled in my spirit by this basic fact about the nation that I love: we are constantly distracted from a problem we could fix by lies that are layered, one on top of the other. I've chosen to confront white poverty for the same reason I challenged that deacon and the congregation I pastored: because *when we face the crisis of poverty in America, I know we can work together to end it.* Seeing poverty for what it is, though, requires a radical reorientation of our vision.

In the biblical tradition that has shaped my imagination, prophets play the role of calling the nation to pay attention to the people they have learned not to see. The prophet Jeremiah lived at a time in ancient Israel when leaders forgot their responsibility to the poor, and vulnerable people were pushed to the margins of the community. "From the least to the greatest," Jeremiah declared, "all are greedy for gain; prophets and priests alike, all practice deceit." The myths that kept people from seeing their suffering neighbors in Jeremiah's time were shared by folks across the society. These lies distorted reality for everyone, "from the least to the greatest." The only hope, Jeremiah realized, was for someone who could see what was happening to stand up and tell the truth. He said he was called to be that "watchman."

Now, a watchman doesn't have the power to enact policy or administer resources that have been allocated for the common defense. Still, a watchman commits to pay attention—to do what he can to really see. And when a watchman sees something that he knows is a threat to the whole society, he sounds the alarm to draw attention to the crisis.

Like Jeremiah, I am haunted by the poor people I have met all across America—people who've taken the time to tell me their stories, just like that woman who needed help in our congregation told me hers. From the suburbs of Seattle to the backwoods of West Virginia, from San Francisco's Tenderloin to the streets of Binghamton, New York, from the hollers of Eastern Kentucky to the farmlands of Kansas, America's poor have invited me into their lives and shared their stories. They have not asked me to bail them out. They understand that the crisis of poverty in America is far bigger than anything one person or organization can alleviate. Time and again, they've simply invited me to see. And they've begged me not to forget them.

In their own way, they've called me to be a watchman. *White Poverty* is my attempt to say what I've seen—to tell the stories of so many in a way that lays bare what they know as a matter of fact in their daily struggle to survive.

According to the federal government, nearly 40 million Americans—11.6 percent of the nation—are poor. That's more than one in ten people, which is not insignificant in the richest nation in the history of the world. But it is a number that we have learned how to explain in the stories we tell ourselves about poverty. And they just aren't true.

We undercount poverty in ways that allow us to act like it's normal and not a failure of our collective responsibility to ensure freedom and justice for all. Without thinking about it, the deacon in our church assumed that a person who came up short at the end of the month had failed in some way—not that we, as a people, had failed her. *How could someone be poor if they were working?* "From the least to the greatest," we've all learned to see poverty this way. Our vision has been distorted by all kinds of lies.

When we accept these lies, we believe the myths that tell us people living in poverty are either lazy or suffering the consequences of their own poor choices. Some versions of this story pity the poor and imagine that compassion toward them would look like mental health treatment, job readiness programs, character development initiatives, or targeted on-ramps to "opportunity." In every version of the myth, though, poor people are a small minority. And whether we're conscious of it or not, the myths teach us to imagine that they are Black, while their white neighbors who are also poor are encouraged to see themselves as "working-class."

In order for most of us to believe, year after year, that poverty is only a problem for a minority of people who can be blamed for their plight, the levels of poverty we name must remain relatively low. The 11-or-so percent of the population that our official poverty measure identifies are the poor we talk about. When government agencies assess the effectiveness of anti-poverty programs, these are the data they use. When reporters write about how changes in the economy impact poor people, these are the folks they write about. Even advocates for the poor often end up citing this data. In truth, however, there are far more people living on the edge than the 40 million Americans our government calls "poor."

According to the government's official poverty measure (OPM), an individual who earns $14,000 a year—or a family of four that gets by on $28,000—is not poor. But try existing for a month in America today on $1,167. If you were able to secure a studio apartment for $800—an increasingly difficult challenge in many, if not most, parts of the country—your basic utilities would cost the remainder of your monthly income. This would leave nothing to cover food, healthcare, transportation, or other basic necessities. By simply choosing to eat or get to work, you would be borrowing from next month's rent—or swallowing your shame to ask the local church for $50 to help pay your light bill. Without the support of family or friends, you would be homeless in a month's time—but still not "poor" according to the OPM. I've met people in America's cities who earn twice the OPM—sometimes working swing shifts at multiple jobs—and still sleep in their car at night because they can't afford to pay rent on top of their other monthly living expenses.

The truth is that our official poverty numbers obscure the reality of poverty in the world's largest economy. The OPM is an outdated metric based on the relative costs of basic necessities in the 1960s. When the government needed a way to determine who could benefit from anti-poverty programs, a staff economist at the Social Security Administration named Mollie Orshansky estimated that a family's budget was roughly three times the cost of what they spent on food—a formula that proved fairly accurate at the time. By tracking the cost of a minimum food budget for any family size, the government has continued to update the OPM.

The way we measure poverty in America has not changed, though, as the cost of housing, transportation, healthcare, childcare, and education have skyrocketed over the past six decades. Since the 1960s, the cost of a gallon of milk or a dozen eggs has increased roughly four-fold. But the median rent in the United States has increased *more than sixteen-fold*. Because we use an outdated measure to assess poverty, we often talk about it as if it only impacts a small minority of people who have not availed themselves of the "opportunities" that the nation's economic prosperity is supposed to afford them. But this way of naming poverty makes it impossible to see that the economy is not working for most of us.

In truth, we have more income and wealth inequality today than just about any other period in American history. While more than 19 million American renters are paying more than 30 percent of their limited incomes on housing, 600,000 people are homeless and millions more live on the edge of homelessness, constantly juggling overdue bills to try to avoid an eviction. This is why, in almost any town in America, you can find a corner of the parking lot at the local Walmart where folks who have nowhere else to go park their cars together to sleep at night. Get to know those cars, and you'll notice them in the drop-off line at your local school, in the parking lot of the places where you shop, maybe even at your church, temple, or mosque on holy days.

Sixty-three percent of U.S. workers today live paycheck to paycheck. The average worker in America makes $54 a week less than they did 50 years ago, after adjusting for inflation. When you think about all of the incredible advancements—or, at least, perceived advancements—in technology that have been made over the past 50 years—computers, robotics, artificial intelligence—and the huge increase in worker productivity that has been achieved during that time, it's hard to comprehend that, when all is said and done, real weekly wages for the average American worker are lower today than they were in 1973. How is that possible? The answer is that virtually all of the economic gains of the past half century have financially benefited the people on top, not working people.

At the turn of the twenty-first century, 85 percent of the total wealth in the United States was held by 20 percent of the people. Meanwhile, a full 40 percent of Americans had no net worth at all. Saddled by debt, two fifths of the country work every day like the sharecroppers of the old South, just to pay bills that are already past due. But when researchers ask Americans to estimate current levels of wealth distribution, we don't have a shared sense of these extreme inequalities. Most people overestimate the net worth of their poorest neighbors and underestimate how much the wealthiest Americans control. In study after study, this is what researchers find: *Americans can't see the crisis of our time.*

Since the mid-1960s, when Orshansky developed the OPM, the wealthiest 1 percent of Americans have doubled their wealth, while the official poverty rate for all U.S. families has only inched up and down. The wealthiest 1 percent of Americans in 2023 owned more wealth than nearly 80 percent of the U.S. population. This radical redistribution of wealth to the very top of our society has hollowed out the middle class, leaving nearly half of the country without language to name why it feels like their monthly expenses are bearing down on them like a runaway train.

America's politicians, like the public leaders of Jeremiah's day, have gone out of their way *not* to name the crisis afflicting nearly half of their constituents. Over the past half century, Republicans in public life have tended to blame the poor, repeating the myths that suggest poor folks are not people facing a problem, but rather are themselves the problem. Democrats, on the other hand, have tried to avoid talking about poor people by developing euphemisms like "those aspiring to the middle class." Meanwhile, people who don't have enough to make ends meet aren't sure anyone sees them. Are they "working class" if they make it to their low-wage job in the minivan that their whole family slept in last night? Does "lower middle class" include them if they sleep in a bed that someone who works third shift uses while they work the day shift at the local factory?

For a more accurate picture of poverty as it is experienced today, some researchers have asked this basic question: who would not be able to meet their basic monthly expenses if they had a $400 emergency this month—an unexpected trip to the doctor or mechanic, for example? Think about the flat tire that the sister who asked our church for help lived in fear of. When we look at poverty through this lens of practical necessity, 140 *million Americans are poor or low-income*—a full 43 percent of the country. This is the definition of poverty I'm working with in this book. These are the data that reflect what I've seen as a watchman in America.

If you disaggregate the data on the 140 million Americans who are technically poor or low-income, 24 million of them are Black. That's 60 percent of all Black people in America—an incredible burden that reflects the ongoing influence of racism in American life, and one that is shared by a similar percentage of the population in Native and Latino communities. But when you look at the raw numbers of poor and low-income people, there are 66 million white people—*almost three times* the number of Black Americans.

Most people cannot see that poverty is an epidemic impacting nearly half of Americans.

And this is what you never hear: *most of America's poor are white.*

I sound the alarm about white poverty because I'm convinced that we can't expose the peculiar exceptionalism of America's poverty without seeing how it impacts the very people that our myths pretend to privilege.

My father, who insisted that I recognize all of who I am from the time I was born, also showed me as I was growing up that wherever you see injustice, you must challenge it. Daddy was a pastor who believed it was not possible to follow Jesus without trying to live out the message of "good news to the poor." As a boy, I remember going with him to visit a poor white family that lived in a little shack in eastern North Carolina. I don't recall what he talked to them about, but I'll never forget looking over in the corner of their kitchen and seeing a stack of empty dog food cans. They had seven or eight children, but they didn't have a dog.

When we cannot see the desperation of any human who is hurting, we do violence to them. At the same time, we also allow ourselves to become a more violent society, putting all of us at risk. A government that ignores 66 million of my white sisters and brothers has no problem ignoring the needs of my Black and Native and Latino kin. This is what I've come to believe as a watchman among America's poor: until we compel this nation to see its white poor, poverty will remain in the shadows.

A watchman has nothing but his voice to alert the community to the dangers he has witnessed. In ancient Israel, Jeremiah wept bitter tears and cried out in the public square. The more I've seen of America's poverty, the more I cannot help but scream.

In 2017 the United Nations' Special Rapporteur on Poverty, Philip Alston, toured the United States to write a report on America's peculiar exceptionalism of having the highest poverty rate among the world's major economies. He visited many of the same places I've been over the past decade, and we met at the UN after he had completed his report to talk about why poverty continues to be something we cannot address in the richest nation in the history of the world. The problem, we agreed, cannot be that America doesn't know how to reduce poverty. Our peer nations in Asia, Europe, and the Middle East have dramatically lower rates of poverty than the United States, and our best social scientists regularly produce peer-reviewed studies that outline policies that have reduced poverty here and elsewhere. Neither can the problem be that the United States lacks resources: we are the single largest economy in the world.

When we want to go to war, we pay for it. When Congress decides to bail out banks, they can do it.

What we lack, Alston and I agreed, is a matter of conscience. Most Americans do not see the scale of the problem. We don't know how to talk about the ways growing inequality has impoverished our democracy. And because we cannot name this crisis, we do not share a conviction that poverty is a plague we must abolish. "I'm not a religious person," Alston told me, "but that sounds like a God-sized problem."

The ancient prophets remind us that, when the people cannot see a problem, a watchman must sound the alarm. Yet our moral leaders have been strangely silent when it comes to the crisis of poverty. Even though neglect of the poor and the vulnerable is a sin decried by Scripture while "good news to the poor" is the very first message Jesus preached, a Pew Research Center study of nearly 50,000 sermons found that neither the words "poverty" nor "poor" register as commonly used in America's pulpits. At just the moment when we most need a watchman in every city and town, our moral alarm system has gone silent.

When we listen carefully, though, we can hear the voices of America's prophets echoing down the corridors of history, calling to us even now. I am reminded of the distant year of 1968 when poor people from different backgrounds joined together in a Poor People's Campaign that demanded economic justice for all Americans. Civil rights workers in rural Black communities noted that the desegregation of lunch counters didn't mean much to people who couldn't afford to eat. And the poor and hungry, they noted, weren't only Black. They were also white families in Appalachia and in the bayous of Louisiana. They were welfare rights advocates in urban centers and Chicano workers in the grape fields of California. They were members of the Apache and Navajo nations, still fighting for the right to exist on their ancestral lands. This patchwork of America's poor was the emerging coalition that Dr. Martin Luther King Jr. was serving when he went to Memphis to stand with sanitation workers who were on strike to demand better working conditions. This is the movement that was building to demand that America see its poor when an assassin's bullet ripped through Dr. King's neck on the balcony of the Lorraine Motel in Memphis, Tennessee.

Just two months after she had buried her husband in April 1968, Coretta Scott King traveled to Washington, D.C., to address the largest gathering of the original Poor People's Campaign that June. A trained vocalist, she began with a song. "Somebody's hurting, Lord. Come by here," she sang, looking out over tens of thousands of America's poor who'd set up a tent city on the National Mall to demand that their fellow citizens see their suffering.

Mrs. King was hurting, but she found a way through the old spiritual to connect her pain with the suffering of millions of Americans—even poor white Americans who'd been fed the lie that her husband was a communist trying to destroy the nation. Yes, her family had been assaulted by a lethal form of violence that stirred the hatred of millions of white Americans before it ever sent a bullet through her husband's body. But in her prophetic empathy, Coretta King was able to see how that violence connected her to other poor people.

"I must remind you that starving a child is violence," she told the crowd gathered for the Poor People's Campaign's Solidarity

Day on June 19, 1968. "Neglecting school children is violence. Punishing a mother and her family is violence. Discrimination against a working man is violence. Ghetto housing is violence. Ignoring medical need is violence. Contempt for poverty is violence."

Like Jeremiah and other watchmen before her, Mrs. King was able to pierce through the myths that keep so many from seeing America's poor. Racist violence took her husband from her, but it did not take away her capacity to imagine solidarity with her poor and working-class white neighbors. Her husband had said as far back as 1964 that "the poor in white skins also suffer deprivation and the humiliation of poverty, if not color. They are chained by the weight of discrimination though its badge of degradation does not mark them." Indeed, the degradation that poor white people have learned to aim at Black people is precisely what keeps them from joining the political coalition that could reconstruct America and end the humiliation of poverty for all of us. When our prophets have crossed race lines to ask America to see poverty for what it really is, they have exposed the myths that are repeated to separate us.

To tell the truth in a time of lies is itself a revolutionary act. But it is not original. Every movement that has pushed America toward the goal of a more perfect union has depended on watchmen—people who see what's happening and sound the alarm. To see the crisis of poverty for what it is and not speak out would be to participate in the myths that hide poverty. It would be to perpetuate the violence that Mrs. King identified so clearly.

When we finally see American poverty for the crisis that it is and refuse to live any longer with the blinders that the old myths offer us, we don't only have the opportunity to see poor people as the human beings they are. We can also learn to see ourselves as moral agents in the ongoing experiment of American democracy. Yes, the history of America, like the history of the world, is filled with stories of powerful people who've stolen from the poor and used their power to pit poor people against one another so the masses would not rise up against them.

Still, that is not the only story. We are also the heirs of people who dreamed of equality, folks who fought for freedom, movements that united people who had been enemies to build a better world together. If we want to change the realities that white poverty compels us to face, we must turn our attention to this inheritance.

Chapter 2

MORAL FUSION

THE WAY TO HIGHER GROUND

W HEN LATE SUMMER COMES IN THE SOUTH, THE morning sun rises behind a haze on the horizon that covers the land like a thick blanket. In eastern North Carolina, where I was raised, we used to go out to the fields early on summer mornings to begin priming tobacco before the heat of the day. But by August the warmth of the noonday sun was so trapped beneath this thick, muggy air that not even nighttime could bring relief. When late summer comes in the South, the only way to get cool is to get up to higher ground.

The summer of 2013 became a long, hot season of struggle in a field more public than the ones I worked in my youth. I was then serving as president of the North Carolina NAACP. Since 2006 we had been building a coalition of justice organizations that were working together to make North Carolina the kind of place where everyone could thrive. From the beginning, we tried to practice what I call *moral fusion*. When we talked about the issues impacting poor people, we insisted they weren't matters of left versus right, but right versus wrong. These were *moral* issues. At the same time, they were not disconnected. Voter suppression that targeted Black folks also hurt poor white people because it prevented politicians from getting elected who would pass policies that lifted all poor people. *Fusion* was about connecting those people and those issues. Putting both strategies together, like my daddy always said we should, we started using a *moral fusion* approach to challenge the systems that create poverty in North Carolina.

And it worked. We became the first Southern state in years to raise the minimum wage in 2008. After winning expanded voting rights in legislation that created 14 days of early voting and same-day registration for new voters, we helped organize a new and more diverse electorate across North Carolina that same year. Barack Obama appeared to be losing North Carolina on Election Day, but when they added in all the ballots from early voting, he actually won, cracking open the "Solid South" that national Republicans had controlled since Ronald Reagan's victories in the 1980s. Suddenly, moral fusion had changed the political calculus in our Southern state. But just as we were beginning to effect real policy change, millions of dollars of what I call "mystery money" appeared and began propping up a new class of reactionary politicians in the 2010 elections. This new Tea Party machine won total control of state government in 2012, and in doing so they began trying to roll back every gain our coalition had won for everyday people in North Carolina.

I'm a preacher, so I noticed when the extremists, who were determined to dismantle our state government, chose Holy Week to pass a bill out of committee that was designed to suppress the votes of the people. Some members of our coalition decided after Easter Sunday that every crucifixion demands a witness. So we walked into the marble halls of the People's House in Raleigh, North Carolina; stood outside the golden doors of our senate chambers; and began to speak out against policies that seemed to deliberately hurt poor and vulnerable people. As moral agents, we were heeding the biblical prophets who exhort us to "cry aloud and spare not" when there is injustice in the land. We were also instructing our legislators as to how we wished to be represented—a right guaranteed by our state constitution.

Rather than hear us, these extremists did the opposite and refused to acknowledge our contingent. They ordered the arrest of seventeen preachers, community leaders, and citizens directly impacted by the legislature's denial of healthcare and unemployment insurance to low-income people. They sent officers to zip-tie our hands, carry us to the Wake County jail, and charge us with violating building rules. When they said our objections were too loud, I asked what decibel level was allowed for protest. They couldn't even come up with an answer.

After we got out of jail early the next morning, outraged supporters asked when we were going back to raise an alarm about the fact that our elected leaders would rather arrest sick people and their advocates than accept federal Medicaid funds that would provide health insurance to half a million North Carolinians. We said we'd be back the next Monday, and indeed we were. Hundreds of citizens packed the People's House as our singing echoed through the building's atrium, and twice as many people were arrested for refusing to leave. By the third Monday, thousands of North Carolinians had gathered on the lawn outside the statehouse in Raleigh to protest the abuse of power. Our crowd parted after hearing testimonies about how extreme policies would hurt real people, and we formed an aisle for people willing to risk arrest in nonviolent civil disobedience.

They processed into the statehouse and were sent back out in inmate transfer buses.

"Thank you, we love you," the crowd chanted to the arrestees. Then, they improvised a new chant: "You're gonna need another bus / 'cause baby there are more of us!"

"Moral Mondays," as we came to call them, were born as a space for citizens to reclaim our government, not as members of a party or interest group, but as people committed to the basic moral values of love, mercy, and the good of the whole. Over the course of that summer of 2013, a mass movement made up of Democrats, Independents, and Republicans filled the Wake County jail with nearly a thousand people. Moral Mondays also brought hundreds of thousands of North Carolinians to do the work of reclaiming democracy in a field where the faces were as diverse as the people who make up the state of North Carolina. Moral fusion began to spread as a way of bringing together the kind of coalition that could compel the public to see the crisis that everyday people face in our state.

Our new group was filled with an energy I've rarely encountered, and the sea of people created a spectacle few could forget. There were doctors in their white coats and patients in wheelchairs who told stories of what it meant for their representatives to deny the expansion of Medicaid under the Affordable Care Act. A mother, who had to remove her glasses to wipe away tears, shared about her adult son, Mike, who had died of cancer because he couldn't get a colonoscopy without health insurance. "And they talk about my son like it was *his* fault," she shouted, her face turning red.

Moral Mondays created a platform for the people of North Carolina to reclaim their voice and call our elected representatives to account for abdicating their responsibility. The fact that millions of people didn't have access to healthcare, living wages, and quality public education wasn't any one individual's failure. It was our shared responsibility, and we had to do the work of reconstructing our democracy. It was bone-tiring work, and I was reminded of those long days in the tobacco field as a kid, when we'd prayed for rain just to have a chance to get out of the scorching sun. But this was work we knew we couldn't quit. The hotter the summer of 2013 got, the more people showed up for Moral Mondays.

When word came that some of our partners in western North Carolina wanted to plan a "Mountain Moral Monday" that August, the timing couldn't have been better. Here was a chance to get to a higher altitude, above the thick haze of humid air, and breathe a little easier. At the end of a long, hot summer, I was reminded of the psalmist who said that he looked up from the desert plains to the hills, "from which cometh my help." We decided then to take our movement up to the mountains.

I have to admit, though, I was worried. Our diverse coalition included a multitude of people from the large, urban areas in the central part of the state. Political pundits often talk about North Carolina as a purple state, split between a deep blue culture in the cities and university towns, and red counties in the rural areas, including the hills of Appalachia in the western part of the state. We had worked hard, as we must always do, to offer a moral analysis of public policy that went deeper than the conventional left–right narrative. But could we muster a crowd in the mountains where the Tea Party controlled most public institutions? And could we rally them with only a few weeks to talk to people and organize? In short, did we have enough fusion in our movement to take it to the mountains?

After some of our partners from the mountains began planning, I got a call from my friend Tim Tyson, who is a white professor with bushy hair and a puckish grin, the son and nephew of Methodist preachers. He has lived his whole life in North Carolina and was serving as the history chair for the North Carolina NAACP. Tim told me ahead of the Mountain Moral Monday we were planning in the city of Asheville that a church out in the hills of rural, white Mitchell County had reached out. Something clearly was going on. They'd asked if I would go and talk with folks about how our movement was rooted in the moral vision of the Bible and the long tradition of moral movements in U.S. history. A diverse city with a state university, Asheville was still an urban center in the western part of the state. But now an all-white church, way up in the crooked hollers of Mitchell County, was asking the president of the NAACP to come speak to them—and at night, no less.

Despite this generous invitation, I didn't want to go. Two decades earlier, I had worked as the director of North Carolina's Human Relations Commission. In that capacity, I investigated civil rights violations and the activities of hate groups in our state. It was dangerous work, and it taught me a lot of history I never learned in school. Early in the twentieth century, I knew, developers had recruited a sizable population of Black workers to mine feldspar and build a railroad through the steep hills of upland hardwoods and pine trees that make up the Blue Ridge Mountains. During the brutal surge of vigilantism-turned-terrorism that Black communities experienced after

World War I, every Black person in Mitchell County was driven out by a white mob after a local white woman falsely accused a Black man of rape. A century later, this was the kind of place where the local meeting of a civic organization often served as cover for a Klan meeting. Many of the men who chaired such meetings are deacons at their local church.

I shared my hesitations with Tim, and given that he writes about history and has experienced such prejudice himself, he told me he understood. That's why he and his daddy, a white-haired retired pastor in a baby-blue summer sports coat, were going with me to the church. I shouldn't go alone, they said, but we had to go because this was a chance to test whether Moral Mondays could be good news for everybody—even the white folks of Mitchell County.

Laurel Ashton, a spritely young white woman on the NAACP staff, told me there were some things I needed to know about mountain folk. These were *her* people, she advised, as she drove us up the highway, and she wanted to make sure they heard our message in language that made sense to them. Laurel explained how to pronounce "Appalachia" with a short "a" sound, as her people say it. And she stressed how folks up in these mountains distrusted people—often well-meaning but insensitive visitors—who seemed to look down on them. Their community shared a strong commitment to take care of the family who lost their home to a fire or a widow who struggled to raise children on her own. They understood this love of neighbors to be required by their faith, even when they knew it would cost them something. As we exited the big, four-lane highway, Laurel turned the Suburban she was driving up a winding, two-lane state road without any shoulder. I began to realize we couldn't turn back now even if we wanted to. The only way out of these hills was to keep climbing higher.

When we got to the Episcopal church with gray clapboard siding, it was packed full of white people. The pastor greeted me outside in the tree-covered parking lot and said he had two questions. First, he wanted to make sure we had *not* come up here to do any politicking. I assured him that we weren't working for any political party. We wanted to talk about the moral issues that impact all of us, and we wanted to examine what the Bible says about how we treat the hungry, the sick, and the needy—those Jesus called "the least of these." The pastor said that was what he was hoping for, so he only had one more question: did I know the hymn, "Blessed Be the Tie." Not only did I know it. I'd grown up singing it at the end of every service in the Church of Christ where my momma, a classically trained pianist, had led the congregation in singing this affirmation of our spiritual bond.

Blessed be the tie that binds
our hearts in Christian love . . .

Though I was far from home, then and there I knew I wasn't a stranger here. With these people who didn't at all look or talk like me, I shared a tradition of story and song that bound us together. "No one who has left home . . . will fail to receive many times as much," Jesus promised. The moral fusion Daddy used to talk about was right here in front of me. I walked across a small, covered bridge into a place I'd never been, knowing I was at home.

After we got inside, Tim's father, the Rev. Vernon Tyson, introduced me with the measured cadence of a seasoned preacher. I began to tell the story of what we'd been trying to do—how we were connecting the experience of Black service workers with white and Latino neighbors facing the same challenges. We wanted folks to see how our elected representatives weren't helping most of us. I then opened up the Bible and talked about how Jesus and the prophets call us to stand with people who are suffering, how they urge us to work together for a community where love, justice, and mercy challenge the vices of greed and division.

When Isaiah says, "Loose the chains of injustice," he's saying, "Pay people a living wage."

When Jesus says, "I was hungry and you gave me something to eat," he isn't just talking about how we treat one another as individuals. He's saying this is the measure by which nations will be judged.

I talked for nearly an hour before a no-nonsense, plainspoken white woman raised her hand to tell me that she and others in the room had been coming down to Moral Mondays all summer, listening to see if this movement was genuine or if it was just a front for the Democratic Party. They were there, she told me, because they believed Moral Mondays included them.

Then another man in khaki pants and a polo shirt raised his hand and said he was a life-long member of the Republican Party in Mitchell County, but he had just resigned. The Tea Party wasn't the party of Abraham Lincoln and Teddy Roosevelt that he believed in, and the legislator they had sent to the statehouse wasn't representing them. Small farms in that part of the state had been sustained for generations by at least one member of the family teaching at the local school and carrying the whole family on the state's health insurance plan. The legislature's cuts to public education undercut Mitchell County, as did their denial of extended unemployment insurance and Medicaid expansion.

When Tea Party politicians talked about Medicaid expansion, they suggested it was an expensive government program that would benefit Black and brown people while costing white taxpayers their hard-earned money. But white folks in Mitchell County knew that many of them couldn't afford health insurance. In fact, more than two thirds of the people in North Carolina who had been denied access to health insurance by the legislature's obstruction of Medicaid expansion were white—people like Mike, whose mother had shared his story at a Moral Monday in Raleigh.

As more people contributed to the dialogue, I watched folks who'd listened quietly lean into the conversation and plant their elbows on the tables where they were seated beneath the large-paned windows of the chapel. Our moral fusion movement had been growing all summer, drawing North Carolinians of every background together on the statehouse lawn. But now I realized it had also energized people up here in the mountains. For years their representatives had talked about being "pro-life" and warned of the dangers of liberalism. But politicians who sowed seeds of division to get elected weren't delivering policies that actually helped their people. In fact, they were slowly starving the local economy. These Appalachian folks were yearning for a better hope, and they could sense that the pathway toward it included joining together with Black, white, brown, and Native people who were struggling in other parts of the state. "Blessed are those who hunger and thirst for justice," Jesus said. Here was a room full of faithful citizens who shared a common sense that they'd found what they were hungry for.

Still, I didn't expect the request, unusual to say the least, that came next. Some folks there in the church had already met together before we arrived. They asked if they could start a local chapter of the NAACP. Initially, I was dumbfounded. They told me it would probably be an all-white chapter, but they knew that what we were doing was right. And it was what they needed. Just weeks after three Black women had responded to the July 13, 2013, acquittal of Trayvon Martin's murderer with the hashtag #BlackLivesMatter, white folks in the rolling hills of western North Carolina rejected the lies of the Tea Party and joined America's oldest anti-racist organization. "We have a saying up here in the mountains," one of the women told me. "Don't poke the bear."

A knowing chuckle rolled through the room, and several people turned to the person next to them with raised eyebrows, offering their personal affirmation of the spirit everyone could feel. Then a woman who seemed like the sort of person who might run the local food pantry stood up impatiently and said, "The head of the Tea Party in this county lives just up the road. Let's march on his house and tell him we're not going to take this anymore!"

At this point, I had to interject some wisdom from the long freedom struggle that these folks were just joining. "Black folks don't march in the dark," I told our newest NAACP chapter, but I invited them to join us on the main town square in Asheville the following day for our Mountain Moral Monday.

Then Yara Allen, a Black woman in an African-print dress

who'd been curating the music for Moral Mondays all summer, led us in singing.

Blessed be the tie that binds
our hearts in Christian love.
The fellowship of kindred hearts
is like to that above.

The familiar hymn's message was never clearer to me than it was that evening as I held hands with white sisters and brothers in that little Episcopal chapel in Mitchell County. The spiritual truth of humanity's unity, which is shared across moral and religious traditions, has often been drowned out by the lies of race in Southern churches where, as Martin Luther King Jr. once said, "eleven o'clock on Sunday morning is one of the most segregated hours." But here we were, after dark on a late summer Sunday, affirming in the words of a shared hymn that there is a thread that ties us together—a chord that, however frayed, connects us to one another even as it binds us to the Love at the center of all things.

Here in a church full of white people, we were experiencing moral fusion. This reality of which we sang echoed a basic truth about who I am. This is my story, this is my song. But it is not a solo. It is, instead, a refrain that echoes across American society whenever we have ears to hear. When Black Lives Matter activists occupied the streets of Ferguson, Missouri, after the murder of Michael Brown in 2014, they sang a song that has become an anthem of their movement: "Which side are you on? Which side are you on?" they asked, and the question rang out from cities across America.

But almost none of the young Black activists in the streets knew where their anthem came from. In the hills of Appalachia, during a 1930s miners' struggle where the Rednecks made a name for themselves, a local sheriff raided a white woman's home in Eastern Kentucky to arrest her husband, an organizer with the United Mine Workers. As the sheriff's deputies terrorized her and her children, Florence Reece sang "Which Side Are You On?" to insist that the white deputies face the basic question of whether they would stand with their own people and demand fair treatment from the mining company. From the hills of Appalachia to the streets of Ferguson, there is a tie that binds people of every race who get up in the morning and strive to hew a stone of hope out of the mountain of hardship that weighs on their backs.

For far too long, we have been divided by lies that tell us Black people are on one side of America's story, white people on the other. And it goes on. Conservatives are on one side, progressives on the other. Poor people are on one side, the rest of us on the other. Red rural counties are on one side, liberal blue cities on the other. But this dichotomy isn't true. We are *not* a nation divided by racial identity and political ideology. We are, instead, a people who have been pitted against one another by politicians and billionaires *who depend on the poorest among us not being seen.*

In the decade since that evening up in the hills of Mitchell County, I've traveled across America to practice moral fusion by connecting with poor and struggling people from every race and region. I've visited a homeless encampment in Aberdeen, Washington, where a veteran named Leon asked why his country could trust him with billion-dollar war machines but couldn't even pay him to flip burgers back home. Leon never raised his voice, but he spoke to me with great sincerity about how it feels to be abandoned. I noticed that, outside the abandoned car he had refashioned as a dwelling, Leon flew an American flag on a crooked stick.

"Why did you hang this flag here?" I asked him.

"Because I want people to see what's happening beneath that flag in this country," Leon said.

In my travels I've wept with a Black mother in rural Alabama who showed me where the sewage backed up in the yard of the mobile home she had been sold by predatory lenders. I've rallied with mothers who were demanding unleaded water to bathe their children, and I've gone to jail yet again with people who were arrested for insisting that they deserve at least $15 an hour for work that keeps their neighbors fed and cared for. I waded into the Rio Grande with a family in Texas that had been separated by extreme immigration enforcement, just to have a five-minute reunion on a little sandbar where they were able to embrace for the first time in years.

In communities across this land, I've had the opportunity to see and touch the ties that bind poor people. These are my people, just as much as the multicolored ancestors my daddy taught me to remember. I have experienced the bonds that unite poor people, and I have witnessed their shared determination to get out of the scorching sun of a plantation economy and lead a movement to higher ground.

Yes, we are a people pitted against one another by cable news and social media memes and politicians who depend on tired narratives to rally their base against imagined enemies of their "values." Yet the tie that binds us remains. I'm a witness that every shade of America's poor has a great deal in common. The billions of dollars that have been invested to divide us may seem overwhelming, but I've come to believe they are a sign of our strength. Nobody fights you this hard if they don't think you can win.

We are, in many ways, a nation united by the shared suffering of a long train of abuses. But when I look into the faces of America's poor, I hear again the words of Langston Hughes:

I am the poor white, fooled and pushed apart,
I am the Negro bearing slavery's scars.
I am the red man driven from the land,
I am the immigrant clutching the hope I seek—
And finding only the same old stupid plan
Of dog eat dog, of mighty crush the weak.

"America never was America to me," Hughes cried out, representing the voice of America's poor in 1935, during the Great Depression that laid bare the myths of America's Gilded Age. The bard of the Harlem Renaissance gave voice to the Black experience that exposed the mile-wide gulf between America's promise and its practice. But he made clear that it wasn't *just* the experience of Black Americans. The solidarity of experience among America's poor produced the shared hope that Hughes taught us to sing: "And yet I swear this oath," he wrote, "America will be!"

The certainty of that pledge—the conviction that has fueled every movement toward a more perfect union in U.S. history—is borne of the hope that is practiced daily among America's home care workers and waitresses, delivery truck drivers and hotel maids. These are the workers we called "essential" during a global pandemic, even though we did not give them the equipment they needed to do their jobs safely or the living wages and healthcare they needed to take care of themselves and their families while they risked their lives every day so others could isolate.

This is what I've learned, both from history and from experience: the very people who have been neglected and rejected are the ones who can lead us to higher ground. "The stone which the builders rejected has become the chief cornerstone," the Psalmist sings in Scripture, and these rejected stones have in fact been the building blocks of every Reconstruction, from the formerly enslaved people who led the long struggle for abolition to the fast-food workers who are leading the fight for living wages today. It's the people who've suffered most who know that we've come too far to turn back now. The only way out for any of us is to keep climbing to higher ground.

My oldest son, who bears the name that Daddy passed down to me, is an environmental physicist who has dedicated his life to building a movement to address the climate crisis. But sometimes he likes to just tell me things he has observed about the natural world. Several years ago, William said to me, "Daddy, if you ever find yourself stranded out in mountainous territory, and you have to walk out, don't walk out through the valley."

I asked him why, and he said, "Snakes live in the valley. You might have to burn a little energy, but to get away from the snakes, you have to climb up the mountain."

"Why's that?" I asked.

"Because every biologist knows that there's something called a snake line. Snakes are cold-blooded animals. They can't live at higher altitude. So if you get above the snake line, you can make it out. It might be hard to get up there, but if you get above the snake line, they can't get to you and destroy you," he replied.

As a watchman in this moment, I know the urgency of our need to climb above the snake line. I also know this is possible because we as a people have climbed to higher ground before. A determination to get above the snake line drove Frederick Douglass and Sojourner Truth and William Lloyd Garrison to work for abolition when it seemed impossible. That same resolve led Ida B. Wells and Mary White Ovington and W.E.B. DuBois to respond to the terrorism of lynching by building organizations of Black and white people to work together to push this nation to higher ground. This is the resolution we need to address the interlocking injustices that lie tangled beneath the table of our common life in twenty-first-century America. "The end of poverty is something to stand for, to march for, to sacrifice for," Matthew Desmond writes in *Poverty, By America*. "The citizens of the richest nation in the world can and should put an end to it." He's right: we need *poverty abolitionists* to build a movement aimed at higher ground today.

When we get above the snake line—and I know we can—we can affirm the basic truth that everyone does better when all of us do better. Public policy does not have to be a zero-sum game, where white people lose if Black people win, as so many of the divisive myths we've inherited suggest. We can ensure that every American has adequate healthcare, as our counterparts in so many nations do. And, at the same time, we can actually spend less on healthcare than we currently do in an unequal healthcare system that caters to corporate interests more than people's health. As we will see throughout this book, we do not lack the policy proposals that are needed to lift all Americans, nor do we lack the resources to pay for them. What's missing is the will to do it.

We can't settle for fighting and bickering and anger—the distortion and distraction of arguments about what parts of history we're going to teach and whose experience counts in public life. When we get above the snake line, we can reject hate and division and the mean attempts to write people out of the Constitution because of their race, creed, or sexual orientation.

If we get above the snake line, we can see all people as God's creation and members of the human family.

If we get above the snake line, a nation of immigrants that sings "God shed His grace on thee" can show grace to immigrants, rather than arresting them for not having proper documentation and building walls that demonize whole communities.

I know that justice is above the snake line. Love is above the snake line. Mercy is above the snake line. "One nation under God, indivisible, with liberty and justice for all" is above the snake line.

When we face white poverty and allow its truth to expose the myths of race and class that have become so commonplace in our culture, we can build a movement that refuses to live below the snake line. If we are to become the nation our founding documents call us to be, we've got to help a new, twenty-first-century Reconstruction grow to full term. We can't allow the snake that's been coiled beneath the table from the very beginning of the American experiment to strike and kill this multiethnic democracy. No, too many have given far too much for us to turn back now. We've got to press on to higher ground.

But I have to be honest. It's not always easy to meet hate

with love. I have learned through a lifetime of struggle with this nation's myths how its lies get down inside of us and stir our emotions when we try to resist them. I'm not just writing about something I read in the Good Book. My daddy, a big, brilliant Black man who served in the Navy during World War II, came home to a Jim Crow South that denied him the democracy he'd risked his life to defend half a world away. He was working to tell the truth and lead people to higher ground in Georgia in the 1950s when a white man put a gun in his face and told him if he didn't get out of town, he wouldn't live to see another day. He survived that threat, but the stress his body endured as he fought against injustice cut his years short. And as his son, I've spent my own life trying to build a movement to get us above the snake line. I know firsthand the venomous threats that spew across phone lines and the Internet in our technological era. I have had to learn how to live in the face of some people's commitment to take me out if I don't sit down and shut up.

No, it's not easy to get above the snake line.

But in that little Church of Christ where I was raised in eastern North Carolina, we used to sing another old hymn that rises up in my spirit often these days. In the language of my faith tradition, it says . . .

I'm pressing on that upward way
new heights I'm reaching every day
still praying as I'm onward bound
Lord, plant my feet on higher ground!

The cry for higher ground gets expressed in myriad ways by people of different faiths and of no particular faith at all. I have learned to know its cry in the determination of poor folk who see that things don't have to be the way they are. No child in America needs to go to bed hungry. No family should have to sleep in their car. No one should die of treatable diseases because they don't have access to healthcare.

We do not lack the resources to abolish poverty in America. We know the policies we will need to implement to eradicate poverty and begin to mitigate racism. But we must learn to navigate a path to get there. We need movements to address the injustices that impact us, and they must include people who've never marched. There must be room for the momma who tucks her kids in at night and prays that, somehow, things might be better for them one day. We need a movement for the father who works three jobs, keeping his head down and dodging every snake he can—wondering before he falls asleep at night if there's any hope of a different set of choices for folks like him.

The good news is that poor and rejected people have always shown us the way to higher ground. It's time to follow them on the upward way. It's time to rediscover that the ties that bind us can lead to a movement that will finally expose our nation's old myths and lift us once and for all above that snake line that has defined our historical past.

PART II
Myths

*A Poor People's Campaign organizer walks with
a resident in one of the nation's largest homeless
encampments in rural Washington State.*

Chapter 3

PALE SKIN IS A
SHARED INTEREST
(MYTH 1)

WHAT MYTH MAKES IT POSSIBLE FOR A WHITE person in Mitchell County to believe they have more in common with politicians who refuse to expand Medicaid than they do with Black folks in another part of the state who face many of the same challenges they do? Organizing people across racial divides to tell the truth about poverty has helped me to recognize a myth that poor white people have been asked to believe for centuries. This myth tells them they have shared interests simply because of the color of their skin. Understanding where this story came from requires examining how race was invented as a matter of law and policy in America.

Race seems like such a given—a fact we know about each person we encounter the moment we see them. Or even *before* we see them. Because race has shaped particular cultures, it can often be discerned by how a person talks or eats or chooses her clothes. By saying that race had to be invented by law and policy, I'm not saying that no one noticed discrepancies in skin tone before race was created to justify human bondage. People caught up in the American story are certainly not the first to demonstrate a preference for lighter skin. But what we mean today when we say "white people"—the identity and cultural assumptions summarized in the term—is the result of a particular set of negotiations between human beings in the American colonies. To comprehend the role that white poverty plays in American society today, we have to understand how the plantation economy that emerged in the Virginia colony created what we now call "white people," and how that identity has been perpetuated to prop up an economic system that doesn't benefit most of us.

Four centuries ago, Europeans who had bet on exploration of the lands across the Atlantic Ocean were in fierce competition with others to see who could get the most out of their new colonial venture. The merchant vessels that crisscrossed the Atlantic both operated on behalf of their investors and sailed under the flag of their particular nation, for example. The *White Lion*, a Dutch warship with an English captain and crew, set out from the Netherlands as privateers licensed to plunder Spanish vessels. Somewhere on their journey across the waters, they robbed a Portuguese slaver of roughly sixty of its human cargo—Angolans from West Africa. The privateers sailed the twice-stolen Africans to the English colony at Jamestown, Virginia. There, according to the record of local colonial leader John Rolfe, the *White Lion* traded the settlers "20 and odd" Africans in exchange for food and provisions in the summer of 1619.

The Africans who disembarked at Jamestown that day landed among colonists who had no reason to think of themselves as white. The Virginia colony had defined neither slavery nor "race" at this point. These Africans—the first recorded in the colonies that would become the United States—may not have been ordinary indentured servants, but they did not fold neatly into an existing institution either. Most Europeans in Virginia arrived as indentured servants, bound for seven years. At the end of their indenture, the colony granted them a plot of land. If the legal status of Africans remained uncertain, their color was not laden with the meanings of race that slavery would inscribe on the bodies of their descendants. Race was not yet necessary. People understood themselves in terms of where they had come from, the languages they spoke, and the gods they worshiped. No group of people existed who considered themselves "white."

In the first few decades of the Virginia colony, servants from Africa and Europe did not see each other as decisively different. They no doubt "saw color," as so many today claim not to; but those hues did not define the power to subdue, humiliate, and destroy. Children of many colors bore witness to the array of relationships among these human beings—Black and white people living and working together, falling in love, starting families, having children, and, regardless of color, held in servitude and subject to the master's whip. The Virginia colony's muster in 1621 lists 23 Africans and a single Indian, all of them counted merely as "servants." These servants of color shared interests—and much more—with lighter-skinned servants who labored to keep the colony going when its prospects seemed dim.

The life of one of the Angolans, a "servant" named Antonio, traces the evolution of racial identity in colonial Virginia. In doing so, it reveals the beginning of the myth that says pale skin creates shared interests. In 1635, Antonio completed his indenture and settled on a plot of land on the Eastern Shore. He married a woman of African descent, obtaining her freedom as well, and later bought other African indentured servants as laborers. The couple lived as Anthony and Mary Johnson, raised four children, and by 1650 owned a 250-acre farm. When Anthony Johnson died in 1677, he tried to leave his land to his children, but the colonial regime did not honor his last will and testament. Instead, they granted his farm to a European settler. The judge ruled that Johnson was not a citizen of the colony because of his color. Race became an identity as the law made decisions about who was not a full member of this new society.

If servants of different skin tones had shared a similar lot when Anthony and Mary first purchased their freedom, what changed over the course of their married life? The court records of the Virginia colony offer some clues. In 1640, a generation before Johnson's will was overturned by the court, a Black servant named John Punch fled his bondage, accompanied by two white servants. When the authorities caught and tried them for theft of themselves, the white men had their terms of indenture lengthened by several years. But the court ordered John Punch, the Black man, to serve his master "for the rest of his natural life, here or elsewhere." The court's decision reveals that Punch's servitude had not been regarded as permanent, let alone hereditary. Decisions were being made to define who could become a Virginian and who could not. By the mid-seventeenth century, the colony was beginning to force Black servants into the lifelong service of a new, race-based chattel slavery.

In 1662, the Virginia legislature reversed centuries of English common law in a measure that makes it clear that racialized and hereditary bondage was their intent. In English common law, the status of a child was determined by the child's father. But in Virginia, the new doctrine of *partus sequitur ventrem*—or "offspring follows the womb"—defined a child's status according to the child's mother. Virginia's population included many people whose skins came in various shades of brown, the progeny of relationships—no doubt both forced and voluntary—among people of European, African, and Native American descent. Under the old law, these children were free, even though not visibly white, if their father had been a free Virginian. But under the new law, a child was only born free if it was born to the white wife of a free man of European descent. This not only ensured that the children of Black slaves would remain "property"; it also encouraged white slave masters to rape the African women they claimed to own in order to pullulate their own slave population. A racialized order of hereditary bondage required a clearly defined class of Black people who could be enslaved. It also necessitated the creation of white people as a race defined by law.

How much did the servant of European descent really share in common with the master who held both him and his Black neighbors in bondage? Shared skin tone may have offered the promise of owning property someday and the possibility of relative freedom that came along with it, but survival in an economy based on staple crops required the same back-breaking labor of the newly defined Black and white people. For many, "whiteness" didn't immediately offer a better life. So it had to give white people a story to tell them that their fortunes were tied to the stars of their masters.

Religion offered a means for conveying the myth. The colonizers justified the African slave trade by arguing that English civilization could "elevate the souls" of enslaved Africans. When some Africans accepted Christian faith, this raised the question of their legal status in the colony. The acceptance of Christian baptism was a powerful symbol to white Virginians, who saw it as crucial evidence of the development of civility and rationality. Since these qualities were seen as incompatible with slave status, conversion sometimes brought manumission, or at least some degree of greater personal freedom for enslaved people. That left open the question as to whether the baptism of enslaved Africans altered their legal status. In 1667, the colonial legislature resolved the issue by Act III:

> WHEREAS some doubts have risen whether children that are slaves by birth, and by the charity and piety of their owners made partakers of the blessed sacrament of baptism, should by virtue of their baptism be made free; *It is enacted and declared by this grand assembly, and the authority thereof,* that the conferring of baptism doth not alter the condition of the person as to his bondage or freedom.

The legislation added that slaveowners, thus freed from the worry that propagating the gospel among the enslaved could diminish their workforce, should now become even better advocates of the faith by admitting enslaved children to the sacrament of baptism, secure in the faith that these children and their children after them would be forever enslaved. As a matter of religious devotion, white Christians came to believe that the economic and political system they were building on stolen labor and stolen land was the Lord's work. By giving it God's blessing, they made it a sin for anyone—Black or white—to oppose it. The religious sanction of slavery included the myth that poor white people were caught up together with their white masters in a divine plan.

Nearly six decades into this project, though, the Virginia colony's racial caste system and its supporting myths were still contingent. We know this because an uprising successfully challenged them. In 1676, Virginia settlers, led by a man of European descent named Nathaniel Bacon, rebelled against the colonial government. While his motives clearly weren't liberty and justice for all, his ragtag army was made up of Black *and* white people, many of whom were servants who could see that their interests didn't neatly align with those of their masters and the colonial government. First attacking nearby Indian nations to take their land, Bacon's band then ran Governor William Berkeley from Jamestown and burned the capital. Having forced the government to flee to ships in the harbor and then back to England, Bacon and his men took the colony. Black and white servants had long conjoined and conspired, but this was a new and dangerous level of cooperation across the color line. The threat of Black, white, and some Native people joining together to overthrow the colonial authorities brought the full force of the British Navy to impose the newly emerging racial identities of the plantation economy.

Bacon isn't a simple hero, and historians continue to debate his motives and vision for what Virginia might have been. He died of dysentery before the British could retake Jamestown, and many who fought with him were hanged when the colonial government was restored. But the response to their rebellion helps illuminate the myth that continues to offer white people a unifying identity today. If the law had defined Black and white people in Virginia, it had not yet made all white people true believers in their new identity. They needed a story to tell themselves why their fortunes lay with the plantation owners rather than with their fellow workers of any hue. White supremacy provided the ideology necessary to prevent the kind of coalition Bacon had been able to rally. It furnished a rationale for the unfolding robbery of racialized and hereditary slavery.

The Virginia Slave Code of 1705 fully consolidated the system of racial and hereditary bondage. The story that said people with darker skin are essentially different from people with lighter skin was codified in law and turned into a myth that would tell white people in a new land who they really were. Americans tend to assume that "race" is something real, an undeniable assignment by the natural world, but history reveals that this isn't true. When we take race as a given, it's possible to bemoan the death machine of the Atlantic slave trade and lament Native Americans' Trail of Tears in the same way that we mourn a tornado or an earthquake—without a twinge of remorse. Fast forward to the present, and we can respond in a similar way to the closing of a hospital or the policy murder of poor people. But this response doesn't make any sense when we acknowledge that race was invented to justify an unequal economy. The plantation system created white people to separate them from the Black and Native people they might have cooperated with to demand a more equal society. Having created a new people, it force-fed them a thousand stories to remind them why being white was superior to being anything else they could ever remember or imagine.

It is difficult for many Americans to acknowledge that the reason for the racial caste system was not "bad" white people's personal animosity toward Africans, as opposed to "good" white people's opposition to slavery. We would all like to think we would have been on the right side of history had we lived through these formative years in the American colonies. But the reason white people were invented was staple crop agriculture—tobacco, rice, sugar, coffee, and cotton—and the desire to make it profitable. Enslaved labor became the engine of the eighteenth and nineteenth centuries. It enabled the colonies and then the United States to produce raw goods at a far cheaper price than products from Europe, since no wages were paid for the labor involved. Racism then isn't an idea that led to a system of oppression. It is, instead, the story Americans told themselves to explain why the use and economic exploitation of Black people was good, just, and even righteous. To get buy-in from Black people's potential allies among their fellow servants, this story had to include the myth that pale skin is a shared interest.

If Virginia's colonial elites invented race to defend their property and privilege, why can't we just shine the light of truth today and make it go away? The reason, as the late historian Ira Berlin explained, is that race is a particular kind of social construction—a *historical* construction. Race has lumbered and lurched forward through time with all the weight of the past as its pile driver. History furnishes no do-overs. So race keeps reconstructing itself, refitting the old ship for new journeys. Race does not hang there timeless as an unchanging fact; it is not an inherent trait that we possess; instead, race is a relationship that occurs and reoccurs between people. As such, even the people who do not benefit from it cannot help being formed by it and passing it on to their children.

Without the politics of domination—without our terrifying history—what we call "race" might become only culture, and hardly cause for hostility. I am not Black, white, and Tuscaroran because of my skin tone. These were my people, and they remain so because I walk through the world with them and they with me. Their songs, stories, foodways, and folkways are where I feel at home in the world. Still other parts of my cultural inheritance, like my faith traditions, my family's love, and the aspirations for justice that certain visions of American history instilled within me, give me hope. Other artifacts, like the institutions that white supremacy built in its own image and buttressed to preserve itself, weigh like a thick, invisible chain around my neck. And some days they render me almost paralyzed by despair.

White supremacy, though, has a history, too. In order for white people to believe that they were white, the customs and folkways that tied them to the British Isles or the French countryside or the Rhine valley had to be replaced with the myth and traditions that united them with plantation owners. This could not be a culture of shared goods since the people who claimed to own Black people did not want to see their personal property diminished. Thus white identity became, more often than not, *a culture of shared fear.*

White people told themselves stories about the imagined horrors Black people would commit against them if they were ever allowed the slightest taste of freedom. Absent any real material interests, white identity offered poor white people a sense of solidarity in shared struggle against a host of boogeymen that the myths keep re-creating. If it's not the imagined Black beast that the white people of Mitchell County thought they were defending themselves against when they ran every Black man out of their county, then it's the dirty immigrant. Or the pedophile in the gender-neutral restroom. Or the communist disguised as a factory worker who wants to negotiate his wages with a union. The myth that says pale skin is a shared interest has a long list of people who are an existential threat to its adherents.

But we must not overlook this basic fact: white supremacy is as poisonous to white people as it is to people of color. It dehumanizes the people it claims to elevate; it uses the very people it claims to champion; and its weaponized legacy threatens to transform the planet we inhabit, if it has not already done so, into a cold and empty stone spinning in space. White supremacy had a beginning, and it will have an end—whether in an empty and eternal silence or on a planet far more just, loving, free, and peaceful than the one we strive to save. The judgments of God are just, but they are not always pretty. Our long-delayed day of reckoning has come, and we are both the accused and the jury. We must decide our own fate in light of the truth that justice reveals.

If we are to be honest about our past, we cannot overlook how the idea of liberty has progressed alongside the racist myths that were developed to justify the murderous sin of chattel slavery. America was hardly unique in its practice of enslavement. What was unique about the plantation economy that emerged in eastern Virginia four centuries ago was neither its violence nor its devaluation of human lives; what was unique was its dual claim that every human being has inherent rights *and* that some are damned to perpetual servitude because of the color of their skin. Racism was the only thing that could reconcile America's excruciating contradictions.

When we pause to look back at how white people became white, it is clear that white supremacy is not human nature. As James Baldwin said, "we made the world we're living in, and we have to make it over again." The legacy of America's fledgling democracy, the fate of all poor people, the viability of our planetary home—all of these matters are bound up with our capacity to change. If we are to choose a better future after 400 years, it will mean understanding that the moral crisis of white poverty that is hidden in plain sight today is not new; it is the legacy of an identity born out of a lie—an identity that has been sustained and constantly reimagined through an old myth that recycles the basic fears that have been with us all along.

These fears have not only shaped white identity. They've impacted Black people, too, and generally every day, well into the twenty-first century. Though my father taught me early on that I had European ancestry in my lineage, I also learned from experience to fear white people.

One evening when I was fourteen years old, I was visiting my uncle Richard, a big man who stood six foot four and worked with his hands every day. He had moved up to Indiana like my father, and when he came back to North Carolina, he was married to a white woman named Joyce. Uncle Richard and Aunt Joyce were both artisans, and they had collected antique windows and doors from old houses in Indiana. When they moved back home, they hired me to help them build their house, and I learned a little woodworking putting that place together. I loved it over there. They had the biggest beds I'd ever seen.

This particular evening, we were watching *Sanford and Son* on the television in their big living room when I noticed an orange light flickering through the curtains from outside. "Damn," I heard Uncle Richard say as he got up from his chair, walked out of the room, and came back with two guns. He handed me the shotgun, and said, "Stand at the back door and shoot anyone who tries to come through."

Uncle Richard picked up a flashlight and walked toward the front door with the other gun in his hand. "Stay down," I heard him say to Aunt Joyce, then he walked out the front door.

I did as I was told and stood silently facing the back door, wondering if I, barely in my teens, was going to have to kill someone that night. Moments later, I heard the unmistakable sound of a deer rifle ring out two times—ka-pow, ka-pow. Then, Uncle Richard's voice: "The next one won't be over your heads."

I heard tires spinning in the dirt before Uncle Richard's gun fired one more shot. Then it was silent. I didn't know what to do. A few minutes later, Uncle Richard came in, took his gun back from me, put it away, and sat down in front of the television again, as if nothing had happened. He didn't say another word, but I noticed the deer rifle was still propped beside him against the wall.

We didn't talk about it that night, but I eventually learned that the Klan had come to burn a cross on the yard because Aunt Joyce's son from a previous marriage, Andy, had told the white guys at school that his father was Black. Now, Andy wasn't nonviolent. And he was a big boy. When one of those guys said something about his momma, he knocked him off his feet. That was enough to get him sent home from school—and to rally the local Klan to burn a cross on Uncle Richard's yard.

In the 1970s, a couple hundred miles and three hundred years away from the time and place where whiteness was invented to keep poor Black and white people from forming political coalitions, I had to contemplate as an early adolescent whether I was willing to kill someone to defend myself and my family. If the myth that united white people used fear as its binding agent, the actions it inspired also taught Black people to be wary of their neighbors. The men who gathered under the dark of night outside Uncle Richard's house did not see me. They couldn't. They could not, for that matter, see Uncle Richard or Aunt Joyce, though they lived in the same community and were some of the hardest-working people you'd ever meet. Uncle Richard raised hogs and traded in town, and Aunt Joyce worked at the local factory. No doubt, both of them had labored alongside some of the same men who joined the mob that came to burn a cross on their lawn. But through the myth that gave them their shared identity, those white men only saw the stereotypes they had learned to fear. They didn't stop to think about whose interests those fears served. As a scared fourteen-year-old, I didn't have much time to think about it either.

It's not surprising then that the myth that says people with pale skin share common interests echoes through the actions and reactions of the violence it animates. While it was invented in colonial Virginia, this myth and the identities it formed faced an existential threat after America's Civil War. By 1860, the social arrangements instituted in the colony of Virginia had shaped a nation. Two out of three of the relatively few Americans whose wealth surpassed $100,000 lived below the Mason-Dixon Line. New York at that time had fewer millionaires per capita than Mississippi. South Carolina was the richest state in the United States. The source of Southern wealth was staple crops—particularly cotton—produced by enslaved men, women, and children as well as their poor white neighbors for world markets. So matchless were the profits of this plantation system that more money was invested in acquiring slaves than in developing industry and railroads. Yet despite this investment, no payment was made to the immense labor force, and this savings to the plantation owners kept cotton prices down. But it also kept prices down for the poor white dirt farmer.

Formerly enslaved people became U.S. citizens following the ratification of the Thirteenth Amendment in 1865. In this new role, they joined hands with white people in the North and South who were willing to see one another as allies. Within four years after the end of the Civil War, white and Black alliances controlled every statehouse in the South. Together, they elected new leaders—some white, many formerly enslaved African Americans. Almost all of the Southern legislatures were controlled by either a predominantly Black alliance or a strong interracial fusion coalition by the end of the 1860s. While their makeup resembled Bacon's mix of poor Black and white people, along with allies who had some money and power, these fusion coalitions were able to develop a more constructive vision of what shared power could look like in a multiracial democracy. It was an incredibly important moment in American history.

These nineteenth-century fusion coalitions enacted new constitutions that promised a better identity for all Americans. They also built public schools and gave all people a constitutional right to public education—something that to this day has not been done in the federal constitution. In North Carolina, the new constitution stated that "beneficent provision to the poor, the orphan, and the widow is the first duty of a civilized and Christian state." It also guaranteed labor rights and a right to the "enjoyment of the fruits of their own labor." When Black and white people came together as fellow citizens for the first time in American public life, they understood that labor without living wages is another form of slavery—not just for Black people, but for *all* people. They expanded access to the ballot and wrote a new fairness into the criminal justice system. This is what was possible when poor white people rejected the old myth and joined fusion coalitions in the late 1860s.

The experiment of the First Reconstruction, however, faced increasingly powerful and immoral opposition. Many former Confederates saw Black citizenship and interracial alliances—these fusion coalitions—as inherently illegitimate, not to mention morally repugnant. They organized the Ku Klux Klan to terrorize white people whom they viewed as race traitors. They attacked Black leaders, and they began to tell a story that would be used to justify thousands of lynchings: political power had unleashed the Black beast, and this mythical creature was coming to rape white women. By rallying to defend white women, white men were invited to initiate themselves into a racial identity through the ritual sacrifice of Black bodies. The lynch mob then offered white folks a way to know who they were and where they belonged in society by fighting to allegedly defend white women against an imagined enemy.

Lynchings were the ritual enactment of this myth through violence, but politicians and other public figures learned that the fervor of the fear that this story conjured could unite white people even against the *ideas* associated with Black political power. Conservatives began to wail against taxes, which had been raised to fund the public education that was benefiting all people. The cry about cutting taxes was an effort to end the First Reconstruction by making state governments unable to fulfill the promises of the post-slavery economy and to lift up former slaves. Reactionary conservatives wanted to keep fusion coalitions from expanding opportunity, enlarging democracy, and supporting public education. They could not outright deny Black people the ballot on paper, but they did abridge the Fifteenth Amendment's guarantee of voting rights through grandfather clauses, poll taxes, and literacy tests. The enemies of the First Reconstruction slowly took over the courts, and in 1883 they would nullify the Civil Rights Act of 1875. By the corrupt election of Rutherford B. Hayes in 1876, Reconstruction was essentially dead. It had been killed by terrorist violence and by the old myth that the lynch mob enacted.

What was the rallying cry of this reactionary movement that attacked Reconstruction? Why were they rolling back voting rights, taking away criminal justice reform, and undoing equal protection under law? If you go back and read the most vituperative political speeches of this era, they sound oddly similar to the rhetoric of American politics in the post-Obama era. Southern white supremacy candidates in the 1870s said they wanted to "take back" their country. They said they had to "redeem America." And by the turn of the century, all of the gains of the First Reconstruction had been overturned. Just as representatives of the Northern colonies had capitulated to the demands of Southern slaveholders at the Constitutional Convention in 1786, Republicans now compromised with Southern Democrats, agreeing to pull federal troops out of the South and end the work of Reconstruction in 1877. The myth of the dangerous Black boogeyman was little more than a fairy tale told by the losers in a failed rebellion against the Union. But it won the culture war for many white people, offering a history that made sense of the Union's retreat and created a common enemy to unite them in American public life.

Thomas Dixon, a Baptist preacher whose uncle had been a leader in the white supremacy campaigns of the 1870s, offered a dramatic rendering of the myth in his 1905 novel *The Clansman*, which became a popular stage play across the South in the early twentieth century. Millions of white Southerners cheered his version of history, in which Northern carpetbaggers tried to strip white Southerners of their land and voting rights, elevating the formerly enslaved into positions of power over their white neighbors. Dixon's character, Gus, plays the mythical beast whose sexual advances toward the white protagonist's childhood sweetheart lead her to commit suicide, compelling the hero of the tale to fight with the Klan to reclaim the South. Those guys who burned the cross in Uncle Richard's yard hadn't come up with their fear-based stories on their own.

The basic facts of the tale Dixon told are almost a photo negative of what actually happened during Reconstruction and its aftermath. Almost no formerly enslaved people received the "40 acres and a mule" promised to them by General William Tecumseh Sherman's field order. After President Abraham Lincoln was murdered in April 1865, his successor, President Andrew Johnson, ordered all lands returned to plantation owners, who were pardoned for their rebellion against the United States and allowed to continue to exploit their former slaves as sharecroppers and incarcerated labor. It was the formerly enslaved who saw their voting rights stripped from them, not white Southerners. And it was Black and white people in fusion coalitions who suffered terrible violence, not white conservatives. Dixon's tale was mocked in the Northern press, but millions of white people still flocked to see it performed on stage. In 1915, a decade after its publication as a book, *The Clansman* became a major silent motion picture when D. W. Griffith produced it as *The Birth of a Nation*. Dixon's college friend, President Woodrow Wilson, invited him to D.C. for the first-ever screening of a movie at the White House.

If the backlash against Reconstruction led white identity to reinvent itself through new forms of the old myth, it also hardened the resolve of some Americans to achieve the dream of a multiethnic democracy. This is when Langston Hughes sang his cry for America to be America again. It's also when religious leaders began to build organizations devoted to defeating Jim Crow through the power of nonviolence. In the decades following World War II, Blacks and whites, Latinos and young people came together and built organizational power, demonstrating their will to tell the truth, march, and suffer. Easter weekend of 1960, Black and white students who'd been arrested at sit-in demonstrations across the country that spring met at Shaw University in Raleigh, North Carolina, and formed a new organization—the Student Nonviolent Coordinating Committee (SNCC)—devoted to building the beloved community and making the promise of democracy real in their time. They chose as their symbol a Black hand and a white hand clasped together, and they organized Freedom Rides, voter registration drives, and marches that defied the violence of both the Klan and Jim Crow law enforcement. The vision of moral fusion had emboldened them to become the foot soldiers of a Second Reconstruction.

With the Second Reconstruction of the 1960s, America saw the desegregation of public schools, guaranteed healthcare for tens of millions through Medicaid and Medicare, and the expansion of Social Security to finally include women and minorities. This moral fusion movement won expanded economic opportunity, the War on Poverty, the Civil Rights Act, the Voting Rights Act, and an increase in the minimum wage. Whites, Blacks, Jews, Christians, and others fighting against Jim Crow in the South risked their lives and faced down dogs and firehoses in Birmingham in order to pass the Civil Rights Act of 1964. After Bloody Sunday in Selma, the Voting Rights Act of 1965 was introduced by Mike Mansfield, a Democrat, and Everett Dirksen, a Republican. Its language was clear: the purpose of this legislation was to enforce the provisions of the Fifteenth Amendment passed during the First Reconstruction. This bill increased Black voting participation and made it possible for Black Americans to be elected once again to political office in the South and join fusion coalitions with progressive white allies. In 1966, for the first time since the nineteenth century, a substantial number of Black people voted in the South. There were still all kinds of problems with gerrymandering and second primaries, but it was the dawn of a new day.

During this Second Reconstruction, there was also a moral commitment to lift poor people, an ethos that seemed to sweep so much of the land. The War on Poverty had three parts: the first boosted wages through education and job training. The second provided income support, particularly for single mothers and the elderly. And the third part aimed to create a system of government healthcare for the elderly and the poor of all races. So while the Civil Rights movement was breaking down racial barriers, the Second Reconstruction was also pushing policy to help everybody: poor white people, women, children, and the elderly. In 1960, before the War on Poverty, more than a third of American senior citizens lived in gut-wrenching poverty, alongside 30 percent of America's children. By 1975, child poverty had been cut in half and poverty among seniors was reduced by 60 percent. In raw numbers, the majority of the people who were lifted out of poverty were white. Ending poverty wasn't framed as Democrat or Republican, left or right. It was championed as a moral issue that impacts all of us. In the language of the Kerner Commission report at the time, many Americans could see that "everybody does better when everybody does better."

Just before his assassination in Memphis, Dr. King brought the moral visions of the Civil Rights movement and the War on Poverty together in the 1968 Poor People's Campaign. In one of his last speeches, King said there's a schizophrenia in America. Drawing on Michael Harrington's landmark book about poverty, *The Other America*, King declared that there were two Americas: one beautiful, where millions drink the milk of prosperity and the honey of equality; but also, and at the same time, another America of grinding poverty that transforms the buoyancy of hope into the fatigue of despair. King used the contrast between these two Americas as a moral framework for announcing the Poor People's Campaign. Such an unequal society did not have to be. The moral fusion movement of America's Second Reconstruction offered people an identity beyond the old myth's fears and divisions. Poor white people didn't have to buy the lie that said poor Black and brown neighbors who wanted higher wages and voting rights were their enemies.

They could join them and build an America where everyone can thrive.

Reactionary conservatives—a so-called "New Right"—revolted against this Second Reconstruction, much as they had in the 1870s. They turned to violence and terror, killing four little girls in a Birmingham church; civil rights workers like Mickey Schwerner, James Chaney, and Andrew Goodman in Mississippi; and many of the leaders of the Second Reconstruction. But they also reworked the script of the old myth. The electoral attacks of this era were developed by Kevin Phillips, a Nixon campaign aide and Republican strategist. He said the secret to American politics was knowing who hates who, and he developed a "Southern Strategy" to persuade Southern whites to leave the Democratic Party out of their opposition to the Civil Rights movement. Republican strategist Lee Atwater later described how it worked. He said this:

> You start out in 1954 saying "nigger nigger nigger" but in 1968 you cannot say "nigger"—that hurts you, that backfires. So you say stuff like "forced busing," "states' rights," all that stuff. You're getting abstract now. You talk about cutting taxes. And these things sound totally economic, but the byproduct of them is that blacks get hurt worse than whites and whites blame their problems on blacks and those whom they are taught are getting free things for nothing.

Atwater would then manage George Herbert Walker Bush's successful run for the presidency in 1988, deploying the Willie Horton ad that used frightening images of a Black rapist to drive home its political wedge. Atwater then became national

GOP chair and worked to develop a solid South where the majority of Southern whites would resist and repel any political alliances between Black and white Americans. Atwater acknowledged that the Southern Strategy originated with the 1968 and 1972 presidential campaigns of Alabama segregationist governor George Wallace. Wallace did not win, but he taught the new conservative extremists how to use the language of antielitism, anticommunism, and dog whistles—racial code words—to inflame white voters reeling, some even seething, with fear and hatred of the Black freedom movement, the antiwar movement, the countercultural movement, and the women's liberation movement.

Wallace lost, but Richard Nixon showed Republicans how to out-Wallace Wallace. Phillips convinced Nixon after the 1968 campaign not only that they would recruit the white South, but that so-called "white ethnics" in the North were also ripe for the picking, correctly predicting, for example, that certain groups—even many Democrats in New York—would turn Republican because "they didn't like the Jews and the Negroes who run the New York Democratic Party." The South would become the base, but the Southern Strategy would be used in the suburbs and across the Sunbelt to form a political coalition of white people who never had to mention race because they understood their solidarity with one another through new iterations of the old myth's familiar fears.

In 1979 and 1980, this is the political playbook Ronald Reagan worked from for his "Make America Great Again" campaign. Reagan had become governor of California by attacking the University of California at Berkeley, Martin Luther King Jr., and the Black Panthers. He'd become a champion of the movement to repeal California's 1964 Rumford Act that prevented property owners from refusing to rent or sell property on the basis of race or religion. When he won the 1980 Republican presidential nomination, Reagan's staff chose to open his campaign in Philadelphia, Mississippi, known for only one thing: the three civil rights workers who had been murdered there. He called the Civil Rights Act of 1964 bad legislation, said the Voting Rights Act was a humiliation to the South, and claimed to have been in a grocery store line beside "a strapping young buck with a fist full of food stamps and a stack of porterhouse steaks." Here again was the same imagined Black beast, hungry not for white women, but for something white men cared about even more: their hard-earned money. Using the dog whistles of the Southern Strategy, Reagan won a landslide in the South and won all over the country.

The men who came to burn a cross on my uncle Richard's lawn in the late 1970s weren't performing the backwoods ignorance of uninformed people; they were acting their part in a story told by some of the most powerful and influential people in American public life. The old myth echoed in the code words of the Southern Strategy and told them that an interracial marriage violated the basis of their identity and threatened the moral fabric of American society. But that myth also served to obscure the ways any relationship across racial lines represents the potential for common understanding that has fostered every stride toward a more perfect union in American history. Fear kept those men from seeing this hope—and because their fear plunged me into a situation of potential violence, it almost hardened me against the possibility of working together with white people. By grace, I grew up in a family and an extended community that prized moral fusion as both our inheritance and the promise of a better future. And in time, I had the opportunity to see for myself that there is a story more powerful than the myth that sustains white identity to prop up a system that hurts most of us.

Chapter 4

ONLY BLACK FOLKS WANT
CHANGE IN AMERICA
(MYTH 2)

I N ORDER TO BUILD AN EFFECTIVE MOVEMENT TO
abolish poverty, we need to puncture the myth once and
for all that says protest, activism, and any agitation for change
are *only* for Black people. Like many myths, this story gets
enshrined in monuments and national holidays. It celebrates
the Black abolitionists and Civil Rights leaders who fought
against slavery and segregation. It creates space today for Black
leaders to address police reform and voting rights in politics or
diversity in higher education. It's a myth that makes many of
us feel good and civically minded, but it is dangerous because it
isolates Black people's struggle for justice from resistance to the
extreme inequality that impacts most of us. Nothing blunts the
force of this age-old myth more than for people of every race to
come together and demand change.

On our first Moral Monday in April 2013, I walked across
the great seal of the state of North Carolina that is emblazoned
in black on the granite courtyard in front of our statehouse. *Esse
quam videri*, the seal declares—"to be rather than to seem."
Our group was composed of Black, white, and Latino; young
and old; disabled and, as the renowned North Carolina novelist
Reynolds Price used to say after he began using a wheelchair,

the "temporarily abled." We had intentionally come as a representative mosaic of the people who make up the Old North State. We were there to be, rather than to seem, a voice for all poor and vulnerable North Carolinians. Though several of us led statewide organizations, we held no elected office, intent that this not be seen as a party-affiliated movement. The moral authority we exercised was the right that our state constitution guarantees to instruct our elected representatives. The force that brought us together was our shared commitment to the good of the whole.

To lead our delegation, I walked hand-in-hand with Barbara Zelter, a white social work professor wearing rectangle-framed glasses and a black business suit. We walked slowly, with intention, past a phalanx of security officers and made our way into one of the lobbies of the building, where legislators, their staff, lobbyists, and members of the media often linger outside the legislative chambers during sessions. With television cameras and an anxious line of officers following us, we drew the attention of people who were used to business as usual in this space. As we walked in silence toward the elevator to go up to the second floor, where the doors to the house and senate chambers are located, I heard a whisper echo off the vaulted ceiling of the lobby: "Where did *they* get all these white people?"

It was an instructive question. I'd learned from nearly a decade of experience as president of North Carolina's NAACP that most people in state government thought they knew how to handle Black people and civil rights issues. The newly elected Republican governor, Pat McCrory, had welcomed me into his office just after his inauguration and pledged to meet with me monthly to discuss the concerns of African Americans in our state *if* I would agree to not criticize him publicly. I told him in no uncertain terms that I hadn't come for tea and crumpets. I represented a coalition that wanted justice for everybody.

I was often welcomed as a civil rights leader by Democrats and Republicans alike to commemorate struggles from the past. And I was invited—especially by Black Democrats—to show up as an advocate for racial equity in education, for access to healthcare, or for environmental justice. But few people in state government expected the president of the NAACP to walk hand-in-hand with a white woman to lead a group of people as diverse as the state itself in an action to demand justice for all people. The question I heard echo through the atrium that day helped me see that the identity my daddy had fought to claim at my birth—the moral fusion he always talked about—was an interruption of the stories we often tell ourselves about who we are in this country.

Those stories, it turns out, aren't even historically accurate. They're based on stereotypes about Black-led organizations and movements that obscure our actual past. The National Association for the Advancement of Colored People (NAACP), for example, was established in 1911 by white and Black Americans who came together to raise the alarm about white supremacist terrorism that was being used to stamp out the promise of democracy in America. Though it has become a Black-led legacy civil rights organization that's best known for honoring Black achievement and hosting award shows, the NAACP's founders more than a century ago were *mostly* white—many Jewish, in fact. Those white folks were shocked that guarantees of citizenship and equal protection under law that had been written into the U.S. Constitution after a bloody Civil War were being denied by extremists who used the language of "separate but equal" to comply with the letter of the law but lynched anyone who demanded equality for Black people. Mary White Ovington, a white social worker from New York who was the first executive secretary of the NAACP, insisted on hanging a flag outside the New York City office that proclaimed, "A NEGRO WAS LYNCHED YESTERDAY." Even if they couldn't stop the extremism immediately, the NAACP's multiracial coalition was determined to bear public witness against the antidemocratic terrorism of Jim Crow.

The power of the NAACP's early anti-racism was its understanding that white supremacy is bad for most people—even those offered the so-called "privilege" of whiteness. Resisting the myths that propped up the concentration of wealth in the hands of a few wasn't just the work of Black people. It was a job for *all* justice-loving people who believed in a democracy where everyone could thrive.

One of the Black cofounders of the NAACP, Ida B. Wells, who was also a friend of Ovington, saw clearly how lynching was as much a fight about who America imagines itself to be as it was a struggle for political control. When she began her crusade against the violence of lynch mobs, the issue was deeply personal: she had known the Black men in her hometown of Memphis who were targeted, and she knew that they had attracted enemies in the post-Reconstruction South by refusing to submit to the second-class citizenship that Jim Crow required. Free Black men who were economically independent posed a threat to the people in Memphis who defended the order of the old plantation economy. Black *and* white people who challenged that order, Wells noted, were the targets of lynching.

This was not the story that was being told in the press, though. Lynch mobs were targeting people—most often successful Black men—who challenged the social hierarchy of Jim Crow's racial caste system. Wells noted that the victims of lynching were never accused of asserting the rights guaranteed to them by the U.S. Constitution. They were, instead, accused of violating the moral code. The story was often that a Black man had allegedly raped a white woman. Because lynch mobs didn't have the patience to wait for evidence to establish the truth of these accusations, Wells devoted her journalistic efforts to uncovering the true stories of lynchings after the fact. Her reporting challenged the myth that obscured the real reason for mob violence that murdered thousands of Black people and compelled millions more to flee their homes in the Great Migration.

Lynching wasn't at all about defending white women against the imagined "jungle" ravages of Black men. No, it was an act of terrorism designed to decimate the political coalitions of Black and white people who worked together to reconstruct America in the aftermath of the Civil War. *Its violence rested on the myth that only Black people wanted change in the South.* More than a century later, when I walked hand-in-hand with a white woman to demand justice in our statehouse, our presence exposed how this myth continues to live on in, even dominate, our common lives.

Here's what we learned: people who understand politics think they know how to handle Black protest. If they can frame it as the grievance of a minority group that bears the legacy of oppression, they have a place for protest that doesn't demand any major reorganization of the way things currently work. But what do you do when white and Latino and Native neighbors begin to recognize that the same system their Black neighbors are protesting is hurting them too? It interrupts the familiar story and makes some people ask, "Where did they get all these white people?"

During the Civil Rights movement, when Black and white organizers with the SNCC worked with local activists in Dallas County, Alabama, in the early 1960s to build a voting rights campaign, the violent resistance of the local sheriff, Jim Clark, drew national attention. Scenes of officers on horseback attacking nonviolent marchers with billy clubs compelled thousands of Americans to travel to Alabama and complete a march for voting rights from Selma to the state capitol in Montgomery. The campaign was a basic struggle for the promises of democracy, but Sheriff Clark echoed the same old myth Wells had worked to expose when he titled his memoir of the events *The Raping of Selma*. If these Black people seized the political power they were demanding, Clark suggested, then the next thing they'd want is to take your white daughters. It was the same old story, nearly a century later, deployed again to persuade white Southerners that the fight for voting rights wasn't their struggle.

The Selma-to-Montgomery march of 1965 was, by design, a refutation of this myth for a national television audience. When some 25,000 people marched up Dexter Avenue to the bright white steps of the capitol building that sits atop a hill in Alabama's capital city, they passed the little brick church on the right where Dr. King had begun his first pastorate just a decade earlier. All across that broad avenue, a full spectrum of color—

Black and white—bore witness to the new political coalition that was possible in the South if everyone could vote. They were a multiethnic fusion coalition—white and Black together—led by clergy who proclaimed that voting rights was a moral issue impacting all Americans.

Looking out on that crowd in March 1965, Dr. King gave one of the most penetrating analyses ever offered in American public life of the ways racism's enduring myths have been used to subvert the promise of democracy. Most Americans remember Dr. King for the soaring rhetoric of his 1963 "I Have a Dream" speech at the March on Washington, but a couple of years later on the steps of the Alabama statehouse that day, he looked back at the history of the South and explained to the nation how the "southern aristocracy" had used segregation to keep poor Black and white people from realizing their common political interests. The monied elites tried to make it about separate water fountains and separate schools. They allowed "vertical integration" in public spaces and designated public swimming pools for occasional usage by Black folks—that is, *after* the water was drained. But they forbade sitting or reclining together, doing everything they could to prevent the fellowship and intimacy that might forge common bonds. Segregation was always about breaking up the political coalition that could change the South, King argued. "That's what happened when the Negro and white masses of the South threatened to unite and build a great society," he explained. His history lesson made clear how the crowd he was addressing exposed the myth that said the struggle for voting rights was a struggle for only Black people.

The divide-and-conquer strategy of the old plantation system, King insisted, was still at play a century later. When Black people in Alabama demanded voting rights—indeed, when they challenged any aspect of Jim Crow segregation—they weren't simply rising up to "get theirs" in a zero-sum struggle for limited resources. They were standing in the long tradition of Americans who have challenged the abuse of concentrated power and worked for a democracy where every voice is heard and everyone can thrive. Black people were not rising up against their poor white neighbors; they were standing *with them* to defy the tired old myth that has been used and re-used to undermine democracy.

I knew we were still dealing with this same myth when we walked into the North Carolina statehouse half a century later and heard someone ask out loud, "Where did they get all these white people?" In the post–civil rights era, the moral narrative in American public life had shifted, but this old story and its tactics of division had not gone away. Politicians no longer find it advantageous to pledge their allegiance to segregation or to use the explicit language of racism to rally their base. Nevertheless, their strategists have found ways to play to old fears and stir up division by talking about "entitlement programs" and a "culture of poverty" in which Black and brown people do not share the "traditional values" of an imagined American past. By segregating poor white people from efforts for transformative change, they try to obscure the fact that poor Black people and poor white people have a shared interest in antipoverty programs that lift from the bottom so everyone can rise.

Sadly, even Black leaders who know the pain of racism from personal experience have often played along with this narrative of division. Celebrating the doors that were opened by desegregation, some civil rights leaders accept the role of spokesperson for the race and work to ensure opportunities for other Black folks to enjoy the benefits of elite spaces in American society. Scores of Black women and men have been celebrated as the first Black person to achieve the highest position in their field. And yet, at the very same time, an anti-racism movement has emerged in the twenty-first century to point out that racial disparities in almost every field are the same as or worse than they were a half century ago. According to the Pew Research Center, the median Black household income in 1967, the first year they collected data, was 55 percent of the median white household income. A half century later, the income disparity between Black and white households had hardly improved at all.

While these data reveal that the success of Black elites has done little to lift poor Black people, it is also true that the numbers of poor white people have increased over the same period, as America's middle class shrank from 61 percent of the total population to 50 percent, according to Pew data. While a minority of Black and white Americans ascended in America's increasingly unequal economy, the lower-income masses of every race grew as a result of policy decisions. The sad economic reality is that many Black leaders have been "accepted" into a system that doesn't work for poor people of *any* race.

The myth that makes protest the project of only Black people focuses racial justice efforts on integration into the public institutions that Black people were excluded from for far too long. But the integration of some Black elites into an increasingly unequal economic system has helped blind many of us to the crisis of poverty that now impacts 140 million Americans. Dr. King saw this, even in the midst of the Civil Rights movement, when he said, "I fear I am integrating my people into a burning house." Sadly, the personal achievements of a few have served to mute the fire alarm that should have awakened all of us.

As the economists Emmanuel Saez and Gabriel Zucman have documented, the ways we account for wealth distribution make America's crisis of poverty difficult to see. For decades, there has been "a large and growing gap between the income recorded in the datasets traditionally used to study inequality . . . and the amount of national income recorded in the national accounts." This is not the case in other wealthy countries. To put it simply, as the rich have gotten richer and the poor have gotten poorer in the United States, we have allowed the very richest among us to hide their obscene wealth. Meanwhile, good union jobs have vanished while the number of Americans working temporary service jobs doubled over the past thirty years. People are working more for less, and with fewer protections. Yet poor folks who face the rising costs of basic necessities are still encouraged to think of themselves as "middle-class" because they have a certain income or don't qualify for federal assistance programs based on the OPM. The house is on fire, but most of us can't see it, even when we feel the heat.

The so-called "privilege" of whiteness has done little to help poor white people whose lot has substantially worsened as the concentration of wealth has accrued to a smaller and smaller group of elites. Yet the myth that says only Black people want change leaves many poor white people believing that this system somehow serves them and their values. Meanwhile, the political voices that blame poor people for their poverty have also positioned themselves as the most ardent advocates for lofty tax breaks for corporations and the extremely wealthy. Over the past four decades, as inequality has grown exponentially for *all* Americans, the number of poor white people—66 million in 2018—has swelled higher than any other demographic, simply by virtue of their volume in the total population. But as long as poor white people continue to believe that protest is for Black people *only*, they remain isolated and susceptible to politicians who blame someone of a different race who is in more or less the same predicament they are.

This myth has been dangerously effective in undermining political coalitions across lines of race and class. Democrats often appeal to Black voters by supporting the supposed "Black issues" of police reform or a national holiday like Juneteenth. But there's hardly a Black caucus in the country that has made ending poverty for everyone a top priority—even though more than 60 percent of Black Americans are poor. Meanwhile, Republican politicians play on the same myth by suggesting that their opponents, who support "Black issues," don't share the values of white people. Rather than pass policies that could actually help poor white people, they fashion themselves as crusaders in the "war on woke" and champion "parents' rights" or razor wire in the Rio Grande to stoke fears about Black people, trans people, or immigrants. In different ways, both parties reinforce the story that tells us only Black people want change. And so the myth continues to obscure the issue of poverty for so many of the folks most directly impacted by it. Because poor people rarely see candidates who speak to them and their issues, they have become among the least likely to participate in elections.

Still, despite all of the lies, poor people who actually do vote consistently defy the stereotypes that are used to characterize them and their interests. The election of Donald Trump, for example, inspired a flurry of articles about the "economic anxiety" that supposedly drove poor white people to turn out for him in 2016 and again in 2020. But exit polling made clear in both elections that Trump lost voters who made less than $50,000 by a larger margin than any other income bracket. Yes, some poor white people buy into the old myth's lies that are used to divide them from their Black and brown neighbors. They buy the story that tells them a Mexican immigrant is going to steal their job or a Black woman on food stamps is taking their hard-earned tax money. But a growing number of poor white people don't buy this. In fact, if it weren't for wealthier Americans, who benefit from the tax breaks and pro-corporate policies of reactionary extremism, many of the politicians who constantly feed divisions would never be elected.

The problem in American politics isn't that poor white people vote against their interests so much as it is that *poor people don't have anyone to represent their interests.* Like Leon, who I met at the homeless camp in Aberdeen, Washington, said, poor people of every shade have been abandoned by America's political leadership. Almost no one says their name on the campaign trail. But how do you represent the poorest districts in America and not care about the policies that would lift your people up? If you're a Democrat, what makes you refuse to make poverty a centerpiece? If you're a Republican, why do you choose to ignore people's real needs—even those who voted for you—and give more tax breaks to the wealthy?

Our public policy is held captive by a bipartisan consensus that poverty isn't *the* major threat to our common life.

Too many of our leaders assume the economy is doing well if the stock market is up, then argue among themselves about whether the market does better when you give tax breaks to the wealthy at the top and let it trickle down, or when you invest in the middle class to grow the whole. But these debates are secondary, at best, when we acknowledge the reality of poor people. Nearly half the country—140 million Americans—know from personal experience that the way things are isn't working for them. But most of our leadership doesn't even see anything wrong with not advocating for the poorest among us. When the media in North Carolina started reporting the story of Moral Mondays, one of our state representatives laughed off the crowd outside the legislative chambers as "Moron Mondays."

In the tradition of moral fusion movements before us, we kept showing up. The old myth that says only Black people want change in American politics too often keeps us from standing together to say, "This doesn't have to be." But when we connect across the spectrum of society and tell the stories of our daily struggles to make ends meet, we can become a movement that looks like the people who make up our states and nation.

We need people in power to ask, "Where did they get all these white people?" When they do, we know we're building the kind of movement that can get us above that venomous snake line. Below that line, there are different kinds of adversaries. In the natural world, one is a rattlesnake. His venom is deadly, but it's not his only weapon. He gets his name from the rattle in the tail he uses to distract his prey so he can strike with his head.

For far too long, we've allowed the old myth's lies to distract us while political leaders refuse to address poverty in America.

We've watched in frustration as our leaders fight over Disney movies and face masks, but we've too often gone along with their easy assumption that the American economy is working just fine and the people who raise their voices in protest are only a small minority of paid activists—or else Black people. I cannot be a moral leader and only stand up for Black people. As a Black man in America, I have to confront white poverty to penetrate the veil of racism and turn old myths on their heads. As Ida B. Wells and Dr. King worked to show us, when we fall for the distraction, some snakes will strike every time.

But when we expose the myth, we can build movements that break through the deadly distractions. In the committee room where the extremists in the North Carolina legislature passed their voter suppression bill that precipitated our Moral Monday protests in 2013, I signed up to testify against the legislation as president of the North Carolina NAACP. While we waited in the gallery, facing the elevated desks where the legislators talked into their microphones, I sat beside a silver-haired white woman who'd come to testify against the bill on behalf of women voters. While we listened to the proceedings, she leaned over to me and said with a deep Southern drawl, "I grew up in Georgia. I know what they're doing. Why don't we switch this up on them? You talk about how this bill will hurt white women, and I'll talk about how it will hurt Black people in North Carolina."

I'll never forget the look on that committee chair's face when my new friend walked to the public comment podium, looked him dead in the eye, and said, "I see what y'all are doing. I'm here to talk about how this bill targets Black people because I know it will hurt me, too."

When it was my turn, I talked about how the proposed changes would make it more difficult for white women to vote. They still passed the bill out of committee, but I knew we'd made the first step toward higher ground. Already in 2013, we were building a moral fusion movement that could see beyond the distractions and expose the old myth that says an attack on democracy only hurts Black people.

Chapter 5

POVERTY IS ONLY
A BLACK ISSUE
(MYTH 3)

I F YOU BELIEVE THE MYTH THAT SAYS ONLY BLACK
people want systemic change, it's easy to think that the
systems of our common life are working for most people. As
with any system—say, the engine in your car or the HVAC in
your home—you can trust this story and still think the economy needs an occasional tune-up. Raise taxes here. Cut interest rates there. Invest in housing or gradually raise wages. You
don't have to think a system is perfect to believe it's basically
functioning. But you do have to trust it's not going to leave you
stranded by the side of the road or without any heat in the dead
of winter. If you can see that a system isn't working, you want
an overhaul. You take out what's broken and replace it with
a new system that works. In our common life, another myth
keeps us from seeing that our economic system is broken and
needs to be reconstructed. It's the myth that says poverty is only
a Black issue.

Nothing exposes this myth like drawing near to the people
who are experiencing poverty. Not long after the sister I met
in Mitchell County told me that the extremist Republicans in
our statehouse hadn't known what they were doing when they

"poked the bear" up in the mountains, I received a call from some folks down east in Belhaven, North Carolina, who said they needed help to save their hospital. In the geography of North Carolina, the coastal town of Belhaven is about as far as you can get—400 miles—from Mitchell County. But politically, the two rural communities have a lot in common. Adam O'Neal, a stocky white man with a Southern drawl, had been elected as a pro-business Republican who stood for family values and economic liberty. He knew there were lots of issues we didn't agree on. But when we met at a rally where a community group had invited me to speak, outside the little city hall, we each recognized that we shared a common interest: saving the rural hospital that had been at the center of this town for more than a half century.

"Critical access" hospitals in America's rural communities were established by the Hill-Burton Act of 1946, during the Truman administration, to provide lifesaving healthcare to America's heartland, where people often find themselves too far removed from a regional hospital to receive timely treatment in an emergency. Because they do not see the volume of patients that has become the norm at major regional hospitals, these critical access hospitals often require federal subsidies to keep the doors open. This is nothing new; their existence has been a justified expense for millions of Americans since the mid-twentieth century.

When Congress passed the Affordable Care Act (ACA) in 2010, they planned for the essential federal funding that's needed to keep critical access hospitals open to follow patients to their local facilities through the expansion of Medicaid. It was, as many conservatives had lobbied for it to be, a market-driven plan. But when Tea Party reactionaries branded the new law "Obamacare," the term itself a dog whistle, they pushed the entire Republican Party to resist implementation of the ACA at every stage. Many state legislatures controlled by Republicans, like ours in North Carolina, refused to accept the ACA funding to expand Medicaid. This meant that a half million uninsured North Carolinians who were technically eligible for Medicaid still couldn't access health insurance. As I'd told the all-white crowd up in Mitchell County, the vast majority of those uninsured people—350,000 of them—were white. But whatever the color of their skin, many of them lived in communities where their critical access hospitals were closing because they didn't have the money the ACA had directed to fund them through Medicaid expansion.

Pungo Hospital, a simple, one-story brick building, sat on the waterfront in Belhaven. In its day, it served three rural counties in northeastern North Carolina. Though the healthcare company that managed it had purchased the hospital from a local nonprofit with the promise that they would keep it open and improve services, the community was outraged because they'd learned that their hospital was slated to be closed. Mayor Adam had already reached out to the Republican legislators who represent his part of the state in Raleigh. "They wouldn't even return my calls," he told me. He was beginning to feel what it's like when people with power believe your suffering isn't their problem. He was grateful for our support, but he said to me, "This is going to shock a lot of people—you're a Democrat and I'm a Republican."

"First of all," I told him, "I'm not a Democrat. I've been an Independent all my life, and I vote like I want to vote."

"Well, yeah," he said, "but I'm sure I've supported a lot of people you've stood against."

"Maybe so," I told him, "but that's not the issue here. From what I understand, you're about to lose this hospital. And if you do, it's going to hurt everybody in this community." We shook hands and agreed we'd fight together in this battle.

If Pungo Hospital closed its doors, the next closest emergency room was an hour's drive for some residents of northeastern North Carolina. "People are going to die," Mayor Adam started saying. We worked with our lawyers at the NAACP and filed a Title VI complaint with the U.S. Department of Justice, asserting that the plan was discriminatory because it would deny Black people in eastern North Carolina access to critical care. But we knew what Mayor O'Neal understood: closing the hospital would also impact the white Republicans who had elected him. The mayor and I went to Raleigh together and held a press conference. Basic access to healthcare, we said, shouldn't be a Republican or Democrat issue. It was a *moral* issue. "Now, Reverend Barber and I don't agree on everything," Mayor O'Neal told the reporters. "Heck, we don't agree on *most* things. But we agree on this. We can't let people die."

Nonetheless, after a short delay, the courts couldn't save the hospital from politicians who would not act to save it. When it shuttered its doors the following summer, emergency medical service workers in Hyde County made a plan for what to do if patients they would have taken directly to Pungo Hospital needed emergency care. Ambulances were to drive them straight to the empty parking lot of a high school, and a helicopter would be sent to airlift the patient from there to a hospital in Norfolk, Virginia. That was the plan.

Days later, Portia Gibbs, a 48-year-old mother of three, was at home in Hyde County, cleaning up the yard with her husband, Barry, an Army veteran who worked in maintenance at the local school. From his riding lawnmower, Barry noticed that Portia had gone to sit down on the porch. He killed the engine and went to ask if she was okay. Her blood sugar had dropped, so he went inside and got her something to eat. But when he came back, Portia said her chest was hurting. Barry called their son to help him get Portia in the car, and Barry started driving toward the EMS station. He called ahead to let them know they were coming, and when they got there, four EMS workers put Portia in the back of an ambulance and got her stabilized. Then they told Barry they'd have to call for the helicopter.

Barry followed the ambulance to the high school parking lot and sat there for more than 45 minutes. One of the EMS workers came out to tell him they'd had to resuscitate Portia several times. They'd called the local doctor, who'd run Belhaven's hospital for decades, to get his advice. He told them it didn't sound good. By the time the helicopter finally arrived, there was nothing they could do to save her.

Portia Gibbs, just 48, became the first recipient of the death sentence that Mayor Adam had seen coming. Despite his best efforts, a white Republican mayor in a so-called "red county" couldn't ensure lifesaving healthcare for a white woman from the next county over because state leaders from his own party wouldn't even talk to him.

Portia Gibbs's unnecessary death was nothing less than a crime. If it had happened because of the unintentional neglect of lawmakers who were distracted by other responsibilities, they would still be culpable. But this was far worse than that.

Her life hadn't somehow slipped through the cracks. We had petitioned legislators at Moral Monday events to expand Medicaid. Hundreds of us had gone to jail when they told us to be quiet. Mayor Adam had come to the statehouse and told members of his own party that their decision to refuse Medicaid expansion was going to kill people. Gibbs's death was, by any honest account, *intentional*. This was policy murder.

The perpetrators, who make the laws, could not be tried for their crime in a court of law. We knew we had to take this case to the court of public opinion. Just as Ida B. Wells insisted on telling the truth about lynching victims, even as the dominant narrative blamed the victims for the violence committed against them and against democracy, we knew we had to tell the truth about the policy murders that were being committed to expose the myth that says poverty is only a Black issue.

Early on a June morning, I rode through rows of loblolly pines on the familiar two-lane highways of northeastern North Carolina, where I had grown up, to meet some folks who had pledged to walk with Mayor Adam from Belhaven to Washington, D.C.—300 miles on bubbling asphalt, under the Southern summer sun, all to tell a different story about why Portia Gibbs had died. When we arrived at a little park on the Pungo River in Belhaven, just across the water from the shuttered hospital, I saw Black folks dressed in T-shirts and tennis shoes gathered with white men in Lacoste polo shirts and penny loafers. Young people who'd planned to walk the whole way were holding backpacks with the essentials they needed for a two-week journey. In the midst of the crowd, I spotted Bob Zellner, a gregarious white man in his seventies at the time, throwing his head back and laughing so hard that his dimpled cheeks buried his eyes.

Many of the folks gathered in that park didn't know his story, but Bob was in Belhaven because he was a white Southerner who had joined the movement for a multiethnic democracy in America in the late 1950s, while still a college student in Montgomery, Alabama. When his sociology professor at the time assigned a paper on the "race problem," Bob went to a meeting that the Southern Christian Leadership Conference was hosting at the First Baptist Church of Montgomery, where the Rev. Ralph Abernathy was pastor. One of the speakers at the meeting that day was Rev. Abernathy's friend, Dr. Martin Luther King Jr., and when the meeting was drawing to a close, Dr. King approached Bob and some of his white college friends to let them know that police officers outside the church were planning to arrest them for violating the city's segregation ordinance.

Bob said he hadn't come to break the law, but to do research for a paper. Was there some way they could avoid getting arrested? Dr. King introduced the students to a woman who offered to take them to the back door of the church while he created a diversion by exiting from the front door and making a statement to the press about the meeting. After she had walked them to the back door, Mrs. Rosa Parks grabbed Bob by the elbow before he made a run for it and whispered in his ear, "At some point, when you see something that's wrong, you have to stop studying the problem and do something about it."

Bob never forgot her challenge, and when Freedom Riders traveled to Montgomery and faced the brutality of the Ku Klux Klan at the local bus station in 1961, he was inspired by their courage to join the Student Nonviolent Coordinating Committee (SNCC) as its first white staff member. Bob learned to use the power of nonviolence to confront Jim Crow because he saw how segregation hurt his Black neighbors. He says he has stayed in the struggle all these years, though, because he came to understand how the politics of white supremacy also hurt people like him.

When SNCC became an all-Black organization in the late 1960s, Bob was the last white staff person to leave. Yet Bob never understood leaving SNCC to be a departure from the work of building a multiethnic movement for democracy. He went to Louisiana in the 1970s and organized white pulp-wood workers—some of whom were members of the Ku Klux Klan—to work with Black pulpwood workers for better wages. Bob knew he couldn't argue a Klansman out of his racism. (His grandfather, a leader of the Klan in Birmingham, had once told Bob he would kill him himself if he protested in his hometown.) But Bob said organizing white folks in the South taught him that, if a member of the Klan couldn't afford to feed his family, he could sometimes see the need to join forces with Black workers in a campaign for better wages. And after Black and white folks sat through planning meetings at the union hall together, it turned out they could sometimes even start to see one another as fellow human beings.

A movement elder, Bob continues to pass on the hard-earned wisdom of organizing, often riding with college students on tours of the South to share stories from the 1960s. He moved to North Carolina in 2013 when he heard about the moral fusion movement that was bringing all kinds of folks together to challenge extremism in our state, and he had been one of the seventeen people arrested with us on the first Moral Monday. Now, he was spending much of his time down here in Belhaven, supporting Mayor Adam and others in the community who wanted to tell the story of how Portia Gibbs, the middle-aged white woman from one of the poorest counties in North Carolina, had been killed by the extremism of white politicians who were determined to undermine the legacy of America's first Black president. Bob understood how a white woman's death in an under-resourced community exposed the myth that poverty is only a Black issue.

As the line of marchers left the park that morning in June 2015, bound for the nation's capital, I stood at the end of Belhaven's frontage road that passed by the shuttered hospital and thought of the funeral processions I've witnessed as a pastor. Whenever someone dies in my tradition, their family and loved ones process to the front of the sanctuary, where the body of the deceased is visible in the casket, and they say their final good-byes. That walk is painful for any family, and I've stood at the head of many funeral processions, praying for souls who are just beginning the process of learning to live without someone they loved. But as I watched Barry Gibbs walk past me that morning in Belhaven, I knew I was watching a man whose grief was compounded by the fact that God had not called his wife home. Legislators who were supposed to represent them had abandoned her to an untimely death. Mr. Gibbs had taken his wife's ashes home and buried them beneath an evergreen in the yard where they'd been working together when she had a heart attack. But he wasn't going to let that be the end of her story. This procession was a form of public mourning for all the unnecessary deaths that were plaguing communities like this one—a declaration that policy murder could no longer go unchallenged.

Mayor Adam was right: some people *were* shocked to see the president of the North Carolina NAACP working with a Republican mayor to try to save a hospital. I was surprised on one occasion, when I attended an annual Fourth of July parade focused on reopening the hospital, to find myself riding on the back of a truck with a Confederate flag bumper sticker. But our shared struggle and mourning exposed the lie of the story that said only Black people suffer if you reject federal programs designed to serve poor, rural communities. We, like many who'd come before us, were experiencing the importance of challenging the myth that lets politicians pretend poverty is something that only affects "those people."

When Ida B. Wells insisted on telling the truth about the men who were lynched in her hometown of Memphis in 1892, she was mourning the loss of Black neighbors she had known. At the same time, she was also declaring that their unnecessary deaths were more than an attack on Black people; they were an attack on the promise of democracy. For decades, from the 1890s through the 1920s, Wells investigated lynchings to unearth Jim Crow's strategy to undermine Reconstruction and maintain an economy that did not serve most Americans. She was a witness to the fact that you can't expose a myth by simply calling it out. You have to help people see the reality that the myth is designed to obscure.

In 1955, more than two decades after Wells died of kidney disease in Chicago, a young Black teen from the same city was spending the summer with family in Mississippi, as many kids did at the time. After Carolyn Bryant, a 21-year-old white woman, accused the boy of whistling at her, Emmett Till, all of 14, was lynched by a mob of white men led by Bryant's husband, Roy, and his half-brother, J. W. Milam. In 2007, when she was in her seventies, Bryant confessed that "nothing that boy ever did could justify what happened to him."

Mamie Till-Mobley, Emmett's mother, did not have to wait a half century to know that her son's actions could never have justified his death. She understood immediately what Wells had recognized decades before: to expose the myth that said a Black boy was a threat to a white woman, she had to compel people to see the harsh realities that the myth obscures. Yes, she had to grieve the loss of a baby she had carried in her womb, welcomed into this world, and nurtured into adolescence—unspeakable grief for any mother. Still, she decided that her personal grief couldn't be separated from the public mourning that was necessary to put a face on the violence that Jim Crow enabled. Her decision not only played a critical role in the Civil Rights movement. It also offered a model for how a moral fusion movement can compel the public to face the crisis of poverty, which is often obscured by the myth that says poverty is only a Black issue.

After her son's body was returned to Chicago in a sealed casket on a train car, Ms. Mamie said she could smell the stench when she entered the station to claim him. But she insisted that they open the casket and let her see the abuse her child had endured and smell the rot that had ensued after his body was dumped in a river. It was then that Ms. Mamie said she decided to hold an open-casket funeral, where some 50,000 mourners in Chicago would witness the swollen face of her boy. She invited the media in to show the world what Jim Crow had done to Emmett. After the funeral, she traveled the country, telling the truth about what had happened.

Rosa Parks heard the story that fall at a special program at

Dexter Avenue Baptist Church in Montgomery. She saw the photos from that funeral in *Jet* magazine, and she said she knew when she saw that horrific image that she had to take direct action to confront Jim Crow in Alabama. What we now call the Civil Rights movement began because one mother took action to put a face on an unnecessary death and expose the myth that said it was justifiable. As I watched the mourners march out of Belhaven that summer morning, I prayed that Portia Gibbs's death might expose the myth that perpetuates policy murder today by persuading so many Americans that the issues of poverty—things like basic access to healthcare—are Black issues and not moral issues that impact 140 million poor people in America.

I realize that some readers might think it's strange to connect the death of Portia Gibbs to that of Emmett Till, who is remembered, along with his brave mother, among the pantheon of civil rights figures. The circumstances of their deaths are of course different, and Portia Gibbs did not face the rank prejudice and bigotry that resulted in Till's murder. But both of their deaths expose a myth, and I want to lift up Portia Gibbs as an example of the thousands of deaths that are occurring as rural hospitals are closed and millions go without access to healthcare in this nation, all because far too many continue to believe that systemic injustice is only a Black issue. In this case, I offer Portia Gibbs's name as the face of all such victims because I know we need a face and a narrative to begin such a movement.

If Till's death became a catalyst for change, it wasn't because it was exceptional. Sadly, the opposite was true: Till's death was *representative* of the violence that Jim Crow exacted on millions of people. For far too long, most Americans couldn't see how "separate but equal" codified a way of life that meant unnecessary violence and death for millions of people. If Portia Gibbs's death was but a single example of the policy murder that was impacting millions of Americans, then to remember her was to ask how we could compel the nation to see what was really happening with poverty. A walk to D.C. alone wasn't going to change the dominant narrative about who's poor and why. Part of the challenge, I began to understand, is figuring out how to shift what Americans think we know about poverty.

I remember when I was growing up in the South in the late 1960s and '70s, that any time the local news station covered a story about poverty, the images that rolled in the background of the white narrator's voice were always of Black people— usually Black women with a crowd of children, Mother Goose– like, standing in line somewhere, waiting for help. This was the era when public voices in the South were beginning to shed all explicit references to racism in the wake of the Civil Rights movement. At the height of America's War on Poverty, it was also the peak of federal investment in antipoverty programs— programs that, by any honest account, significantly improved the lives of Black and white Americans. But at precisely the moment when more white Americans than ever before were receiving federal help to climb out of poverty through Head Start vouchers, Medicaid for their children, food stamps, and the Earned Income Tax Credit (EITC), we were trained by the media to imagine poverty as a Black problem. The public was falsely led to believe that antipoverty programs only benefited Black people. Tragically, this fallacy persists to this day.

Such racist depictions were not always the case. During the Great Depression, when economic hardship touched so many

Americans' lives, images of "hobos" riding the rails, men standing in bread lines, and poor women struggling to feed their children were overwhelmingly pictures of white people. President Franklin Delano Roosevelt's administration commissioned photographers to document poverty for the Federal Resettlement Administration (later called the Farm Security Administration). In 1936, Dorothea Lange, a white woman originally from New Jersey, took her camera into a pea field in California and spotted Florence Owens Thompson, a mother of seven who sat chin-in-hand with a furrowed brow, her children clinging to her tattered clothes underneath a makeshift tent. "I saw and approached the hungry and desperate mother," Lange later wrote, "as if drawn by a magnet. I do not remember how I explained my presence or my camera to her, but I do remember she asked me no questions." Lange titled the series of five exposures she made that day "Migrant Mother." This picture of a woman who looked white became *the* iconic image of the Great Depression in textbooks and public memorials. Still ninety or so years ago, American poverty was the plight of a white mother who'd fallen on hard times, and the imagery depicting American poverty remained persistently white.

After the Civil Rights Act of 1964 and the Fair Housing Act of 1968, which ensured access to antipoverty programs for nonwhite Americans, the public face of poverty began to change dramatically. At the moment when we as a nation made our greatest push to expand efforts to include everyone, politicians who opposed those programs began to vilify the poor people who benefited from them. To do so, they leaned into the old myth. They effectively erased a huge swath of the white poor and created the stereotype of a Black "welfare queen."

Beginning with his 1976 campaign for president, the former actor Ronald Reagan began citing the tale of a Black woman from Chicago who drove a Cadillac to the welfare office and defrauded honest taxpayers of their hard-earned money. While white Americans were doing their best to take care of their families and share with their neighbors out of the generosity of their hearts, they learned from Reagan that a Black woman was using the government to pick their pocket. If they elected him, he promised, the government would stop helping Black people steal from them.

Reagan's mythological Black boogeywoman was, in fact, based on an actual case of a con artist, who sometimes went under the name Linda Taylor. Reagan had learned about her not because the government was facilitating her crimes, but rather because the *Chicago Tribune* reported at the time about how the government was prosecuting Taylor. A different storyteller might just as easily have emphasized the ways Taylor's fraud stole from the poor people who *did* qualify for the government programs she had scammed. Instead, Reagan used her as an anecdote to undermine programs that had helped many of the hardworking, everyday Americans whose votes he sought.

The myth that says that poverty is a Black issue obscures the fact that white folks are potentially the single largest base for a movement of poor people that could demand our government address the crisis of poverty in America. The perpetuation of the Black-only poverty myth allows politicians to pretend that the system is basically working for most people—that if the economy is growing, we'll all benefit from a "trickle-down" soon enough. When poor white people experience the daily struggle that suggests things aren't working for them, this same myth suggests that someone else is to blame. As long as Americans can be divided by identity politics and cultural wedge issues, there is not a single political coalition that has the power to change how we think about poverty and, thus, what we can do about it. But when poor white people begin to see how their own well-being is tied up with the fortunes of other poor people, they and their allies—all who care about the common good—become an overwhelming majority of the American population.

It's sadly true that we couldn't save Pungo Hospital. Bulldozers leveled the little brick building where almost every baby in three counties had been delivered for decades, in order to make room for waterfront condos. But that community's determination to share Portia Gibbs's story echoed the wisdom of Ida Wells, even Mamie Mobley, and almost every other movement that's been able to shatter age-old myths in order to reconstruct America. When we help people see the real pain that people are suffering, it can indeed break the spell of the myths that blind us.

A white woman now lies buried in Hyde County. I maintain that she is a powerful example that poverty isn't just a Black issue. It's *the* justice issue that every American must face.

Chapter 6

WE CAN'T OVERCOME
DIVISION
(MYTH 4)

H ISTORY MAKES CLEAR THAT THE DIVISION WE
face in American politics today isn't new. Yes, the current potential for an electorate that could bring about transformative change has animated an extreme backlash against
fusion movements and the promises of democracy. But as we've
seen, this isn't new either. In times of heightened tension, the
vested interests of an unequal society repackage America's old
myths to crack coalitions that could effect change and to isolate
individuals. Yet another myth is repeated to quash the hopes
of all who yearn for change. It says that any attempt to build a
more perfect union with liberty and justice for all is just wishful thinking. Resistance is futile, this myth whispers in myriad
ways. Its constant mantra, like a siren's song, is that we can't
overcome our divisions.

At our last Moral Monday in the summer of 2013, I remember finishing a cable news interview on the statehouse lawn after
our rally and action had ended. Whenever the media wanted to
talk to me about the movement, I always invited a sampling of
the crowd to stand with me so the television audience could see
the diversity of our coalition. When we finished that August
evening, I was soaking wet. My body clearly needed some rest.

But in the group that had stood together for the interview, I spotted a young woman coming my way. I noticed that she happened to be wearing all black.

I could tell she had something to say, but I wasn't sure I had the strength to listen. Still, I greeted her and leaned on my cane as she began to speak. "I just wanted to say thank you," she said, quiet and a little nervous, but gaining courage as she put her words together. "I grew up in a really conservative church, and I haven't been to anything religious in years. But I've been here every week this summer, and I really needed this . . . I think I needed it for the cleansing of my soul."

I asked her what she meant, and she told me about how, growing up in a Southern Baptist church, she'd learned that gay people and liberals were a threat to her values. People who worked for civil rights and human rights were also suspect because they might be communists. She hadn't entirely understood it at the time, but all the old myths used to divide people in America had been presented to her in the guise of Christian faith. "But over these past thirteen weeks," she said to me, "I've been able to see everything I was taught to despise."

She wanted to say thank you because she'd witnessed what she'd learned to fear, and it had nurtured in her a seed of hope. Maybe it was possible for people to come together and unite around love, mercy, and justice. My body still needed rest, but that young woman's testimony restored my spirit.

That winter, I took a short sabbatical to discern what was happening around me and what my role should be in nurturing the hope that that young woman and so many others were experiencing. Union Seminary in New York City had offered me a modest apartment where I could get away. I looked forward to spending a couple of months reading history, meditating on the Scriptures that I've preached my whole adult life, and having quiet conversations with economists and Bible scholars, sociologists and theologians. I thought a lot about the struggles that we'd faced to bring together a fusion coalition as the Forward Together Moral Movement—not just opposition from without, but also resistance from within. Long before reactionary politicians began to fight us in public, I had struggled with factions within the North Carolina NAACP that didn't want to work with others or expand our work for justice beyond a narrow set of "Black issues." Before we ever got started with the idea of bringing together a statewide moral fusion coalition, I almost got shut down by a faction within the executive committee that communicated this wasn't how the NAACP did things. Those folks resisted expanding the vision of our work, but a wise elder in that first meeting spoke up and said, "Don't you think we should at least hear the vision of the new president that our branches just elected?" Rather than ask the committee to approve it, he called for a vote of confidence for the "spirit of the vision." We didn't have to have everyone on board, he understood. We just had to find a way to move forward together.

I mused on all that we'd learned and tried to remain open to where it might be leading me as a pastor, as a civil rights leader, and as a human being. But my meditations kept bringing me back to that young white woman, clad in black, who'd stopped me to share her hope. I'm not sure why she wore black, but I sensed she had been in mourning for some time. She knew the religion she was raised on had become deeply problematic. It kept the old myths alive, but it didn't offer her a life she wanted.

It was not only killing the promises of democracy, but it was also separating her from people she loved and the community in which she was raised. In my spirit, I understood that she had been courageous and honest enough about the existential dilemma she was caught up in to walk away from her faith community. When she'd walked into Moral Mondays, she'd seen that something else was possible. She had received, as the Bible says, "a crown of beauty instead of ashes, the oil of joy instead of sorrow." She'd shared that joy with me at a moment when I was physically exhausted; and I couldn't forget the way her experience dispelled the myth that says we cannot overcome our divisions.

At the end of that sabbatical, I sensed a clear direction for my own work: if America was to become a nation where all of its people can thrive, we needed a renaissance for the twenty-first century of the moral fusion movements that powered the nation's First and Second Reconstructions. No one person or organization could make that happen, but I gained some clarity: I could preach the hope of a Third Reconstruction to the nation, and I could share what we'd learned about how to build moral fusion movements during Moral Mondays.

I started writing a book called *The Third Reconstruction*, and I planned to preach "Moral Revivals" in seven U.S. cities with fellow preachers who were Black and white, male and female, Christian and Jewish, gay and straight. For over a decade, the state chapter of the NAACP had been able to hold the work of building a moral fusion movement in North Carolina, but to take this vision to other states and get beyond the familiar assumption that a Black civil rights leader was only trying to fight for "Black issues," I needed to establish a new institutional home—a vision that had been growing within me for several years.

In the writings of the prophet Isaiah, I found an ancient mandate for the work I knew we were called to do. "If you take away from the midst of you the yoke, the pointing of the finger, and speaking wickedness," the prophet declared, "your ancient ruins shall be rebuilt; you shall raise up the foundations of many generations; you shall be called the repairer of the breach." If we did what we could do, I heard God saying through the prophet, then our efforts would connect with others who were doing what they could to catalyze a movement that would bring people together from every walk of life to reclaim the promise of "liberty and justice for all." The prophet didn't say that everybody had to change—he didn't even say it would require a majority. If just some of us who understood the forces at work to divide us committed to become repairers of the breach, it would be enough to "raise up the foundations" that our foremothers and forefathers before us had built. We launched a new national social justice organization and named it Repairers of the Breach.

The prophetic notion of a "remnant"—a small number of committed individuals—that can shift the conscience of a nation is always counterintuitive, but it seemed crazy to many people in 2016, as then-candidate Donald Trump's rallies dominated the headlines. If I closed my eyes when I was listening to the news, I felt like I was hearing George Wallace when he ran for president in 1968, railing against "anarchists" and "communists" to excite old fears, all the while promising "law and order" to soothe their anxious souls. The old myths echoed louder than ever. At a rally in Fayetteville, North Carolina, a young Black man stood up to protest Trump's explicit racism. As he was being escorted out by security, Trump shouted, "Get him outta here!" A rallygoer stepped into the aisle and sucker-punched the protestor in the face. Trump told the press he'd pay the assailant's legal bills. If anything was shifting the public narrative, it seemed to be the frontrunner for the Republican nomination for president, who was discarding the dog whistles and shouting the Southern Strategy's messaging through a bullhorn.

That was only one side of the story, though. For every action in public life, there is an opposite reaction. If extremism dominated the headlines, the conversation around millions of kitchen tables, water coolers, and fellowship halls was about where all this anger and hatred was coming from. When we began our Moral Revival tour in 2016, there wasn't a meeting where the church or synagogue wasn't packed with people eager to hear the vision for a moral fusion movement. We had planned for seven cities, but groups in other states kept calling to ask if we could add another stop to the tour. The night we were at Bethel AME Church in Boston, I remember driving up to the old stone building and seeing a line of people that wrapped around the block. Folks waited over an hour to get into an overflow room so they could hear about something that might unite the country. Yes, the old myth's divide-and-conquer tactics were on full display. At the same time, Americans' hunger for a movement that could bring us together was also.

At our Moral Revivals we practiced what we'd learned through Moral Mondays: this wasn't just a platform for speakers and preachers to cast a vision. We were building a stage for everyday people to tell their own stories and explain why the systems that we too often accept weren't working for them. Divide-and-conquer strategies appeal to people who are angry by giving them someone to blame. But we understood that tens of millions of poor and working people are angry for good reason. A mother who'd served food all day at McDonald's told the crowd at Bethel AME that she couldn't feed her own children without food stamps, and her family couldn't afford a place to stay in Boston with the money she earned at little more than the minimum wage. We weren't in the South, and this wasn't a so-called "red county." But poor people of every hue were struggling to make it here just like they were everywhere else in the country. As they lifted up their testimonies beneath the dark wooden beams of that hallowed space, I looked up and felt as if I were inside a ship. Each of us might have come to that place shaped by different stories, but we knew as we listened that we were in the same boat now.

By the summer of 2016, our Moral Revival tour had taken a "Higher Ground Moral Agenda," outlining moral policies that would lift all poor and working people, to both the Republican and the Democratic national conventions. When a white man on our staff at Repairers of the Breach stopped by the RNC headquarters to say that a group of clergy wanted to deliver a moral agenda, he got an enthusiastic response. The folks he talked to assumed we were a religious right organization, there to echo their talking points about "traditional values." When we showed up with an agenda to lift poor Americans, they threatened to have us arrested if we didn't leave immediately.

Before we took the same agenda to DNC officials in Philadelphia, a representative called to ask if I would address their convention on the evening they were scheduled to nominate Hillary Clinton as their candidate for president. At first, I declined. Our moral fusion movement was not about endorsing any party or candidate; our aim was to fundamentally shift the moral narrative in the nation and compel all politicians to face the reality of poverty in America. When they called back a second time, I told them I would go if I could deliver the message I had been preaching at the Moral Revivals. After hearing scores of testimonies from everyday people who were struggling to get by in more than two dozen cities, I had begun to turn night after night to the prophetic diagnosis that, when the vulnerable are suffering, it is a sign that the society is not well. For months I'd been proclaiming that we had a heart problem in America. When the DNC finally agreed to let me carry this message to their convention, I ended up preaching the hope of moral fusion to 60 million Americans on prime-time television.

"Our deepest moral traditions are clear that the only thing which makes a nation exceptional is the way she cares for the least of these," I said as I stood on the stage of the convention hall that evening. "When we witness attempts to forsake our moral traditions and use religion to camouflage meanness, we know we have a heart problem in America." The diagnosis was critical: the source of strife and division in our common life wasn't simply political enemies that could be defeated at the ballot box. It was our collective abandonment of tens of millions of poor and working people, our failure to protect voting rights for all Americans, our neglect of children in communities where public schools had been hollowed out. It was a difficult diagnosis to hear, especially on a night when a party was trying to celebrate its nominee. But an honest diagnosis made it possible to proclaim the cure that can overcome our divisions.

"We know there have always been forces that want to harden—even stop—the heart of our democracy," I preached. "But there have also always been people who stood together to stir what Sister Dorothy Day called 'a revolution of the heart'—a revolution that must begin with each one of us." I had used up the time that was allotted and the teleprompter went blank, but everyone in that convention hall was on their feet, as hungry for hope as the young woman in black who'd greeted me on the Halifax Mall in Raleigh. "When my daddy used to hold revival services, he would cry out to the God who is a 'heart fixer and a mind regulator,'" I told the people who were lifting their hands to receive this vision, some with tears in their eyes. "So I just stopped by this evening to say that if we're going to push toward a more perfect union we need a heart fixing. . . . We are being called like our forefathers and foremothers to be the moral defibrillators of our time."

I could no longer hear myself over the roar of the crowd. I walked backstage and almost bumped into a white woman who was walking straight toward me. She had been crying so hard that I could see the mascara from her eyelashes running down her cheeks. She fell into my shoulder and kept crying. All she could say was, "Thank you." She wasn't wearing black—she was dressed up to entertain the nation. But the hope that we might find a way to overcome our divisions had touched something deep inside of her as well.

I've been a preacher long enough to know that the measure of a sermon isn't how many people come to listen or how much praise you receive afterward; the measure of the preached Word is the action it inspires in the lives of people who receive its vision and begin to put it into practice. My prayer since 2016 has been that all of the movements that have risen up in response to injustice in America would flow together into something larger than any of us could plan or imagine. If people fighting for a living wage could link up with people fighting for voting rights; if young folks fighting for climate action could link up with folks trying to pass common-sense gun control; if immigrants struggling to keep their families together could connect with unhoused people fighting for a place to be; if Native elders and youth protecting the water could link up with people in cities who can buy unleaded gas but can't get unleaded water; if people who don't think of themselves as political but are fed up with the way things are could link up with the movements that have been pushing for policies that could change the daily reality for most of us—if all of us could get together, that would be a mighty force for change.

If we know our history, we know that we are at a critical juncture; that this is a moment of great potential—and one fraught with dangers both visible and lurking underneath. Yes, we're more divided than ever. And, at the same time, there's more hunger for moral fusion movements than I've experienced in my lifetime. It is, as the novelist Charles Dickens said, both "the best of times and the worst of times." In moments like this, when we're caught in the tension between the potential for transformation and the backlash against it, we're vulnerable to the myth that says we can't overcome our divisions. Those who profit from preventing moral fusion movements do everything in their power to make division seem inevitable. In times like these, it's critical to remember the movements that have enabled every stride toward freedom in our nation's history. Poor and hurting people have been at the heart of every one of those movements.

I've been to some inspiring gatherings over the past several years where I've sensed that the pressure is building for a new kind of coming together that is so desperately needed. But it's not the big conventions and marches that keep my hope alive. It's the work I've seen in places where people who are directly impacted by poverty are taking collective action to build the sort of moral fusion coalition we need to reconstruct an economy that will work for all of us.

In 2018, precisely fifty years after welfare rights organizers, labor activists, and civil rights workers brought Black, white, Latino, and Native people together for a Poor People's Campaign in America, our team at Repairers of the Breach helped relaunch their effort as a twenty-first-century campaign to build a moral fusion movement for a Third Reconstruction in America. We didn't do it alone. I talked with my dear white sister Liz Theoharis, who wears the spectacles of a scholar, the robe of a preacher, and the shoes of someone who has walked with poor communities for decades. Liz directs the Kairos Center at Union Theological Seminary, which works to highlight and teach the wisdom of poor people's movements. "If we're going to take up the Poor People's Campaign," I said, "we've got to have fusion throughout." Liz agreed, and our organizations partnered to relaunch the campaign as a national call for moral revival with cochairs—one Black, one white; one male, one female; one from the South, and one from the North.

On the fiftieth anniversary of Dr. King's assassination, we

went to Memphis, where Dr. King was gunned down while standing with sanitation workers, and I spoke from the same balcony where he was standing when an assassin's bullet ripped through his neck. "By the time Dr. King got to Memphis," I reminded the crowd that stretched from the parking lot of the Lorraine Motel into Mulberry Street, "he was hated by racists, moderates, politicians, a president, and even jealous Black leaders who used his position against the Vietnam War as an excuse to diminish his status in the eyes of liberal white America. And then the shot rang out. And his body fell." I was standing with Liz and others right where the blood had pooled as the life flowed out of Dr. King's body. And I remembered what Jesus said when he declared, "Woe unto those who honor the tombs of the prophets."

We did not need another commemoration, I declared. We needed a re-*consecration*—a renewed commitment to build the movement that can change the conversation about what is possible in our life together. "You don't honor a prophet by celebrating his death. No, if you want to honor him, you reach down into the blood, where his baton fell, and you pick it up to carry it the next leg of the race."

If the Southern Strategy had gone directly to poor white Southerners, using the language of their faith to exploit their darkest fears, then a moral fusion movement must have the courage and the vision to connect with poor white people as well. If we were going to take up the baton of the Poor People's Campaign, we had to take what we'd learned in Mitchell County and Belhaven and make it accessible to everyday folks who'd been told all of their lives that allegiance to God, family, and country meant voting for the guy who said he'd make it easier to get a gun.

If I knew nothing else, I knew that white people did not believe these things because they were stupid. People who work every day to feed their communities, clean buildings, care for the vulnerable, take out the trash, fix the machines we all use, run supply chains, and keep this country running are, mind you, not dumb. Americans rely on poor people for our most basic needs, but poor folks know from experience that most people do not respect their wisdom or their work. To be poor in America is to be told that you are a failure after you've worked overtime to take care of yourself and your family as well as your wealthier neighbors. All across America, I've met mothers— Black, white, and brown—who could balance their town's budget on the back of an envelope. They know how to quickly account for assets and liabilities, and they are adept at prioritizing the things that make survival possible. Whatever poor people believe about why their lives are difficult, the problem, I must emphasize, is not their ignorance.

Even intelligent people, though, can be persuaded by the myth that says we can't overcome our divisions—especially when they are inundated with manufactured mean-spiritedness. Nancy MacLean, a historian at Duke University who became a dear friend of Moral Mondays, wrote a book called *Democracy in Chains* that helped me understand how white people were persuaded to both believe the lies of the Southern Strategy and, at the very same time, think that race has nothing to do with it. Reactionary conservatives understood after the 1960s that it was important not to appear racist. Beware then, I say, of Trojan horses. In the case of the new agents of division, they showed up for Martin Luther King Day celebrations, adopted the language of diversity, and actively recruited Black conservatives to repeat their talking points in public life. Strict racial segregation was no longer necessary if the old fears that had separated Black and white people for centuries could be tapped in other ways. By sorting through the papers of an influential neoliberal economist, MacLean was able to chronicle how reactionary conservatives built a narrative to justify an economy that would undercut the majority of Americans.

While the Southern Strategy was able to tap the antigovernment sentiments of Southerners who were angry about the expansion of civil rights and liberties for nonwhite people, women, and the LGBTQ community, most Americans still valued the public goods and benefits that the federal government had made available in the twentieth century: high-quality public education, Social Security, unemployment insurance, Medicare, Medicaid, and environmental protection. From the Progressive Era through the New Deal, these public goods were restricted by explicit racial exclusion, but the wins of the Civil Rights movement made many of them available to Blacks and whites alike, though still in varying degrees. Nevertheless, these public goods enjoyed bipartisan support and were widely popular—the sort of things Americans associated with what it meant to live in the "land of the free and the home of the brave." While individual liberty and self-reliance have always been American values, liberty for much of the twentieth century also meant the freedom to access some basic necessities that were increasingly available to everyone.

All of these things are costly, though, and a political movement that wanted to cut taxes had to figure out a way to cut costs. To do so, MacLean explains, they sought ways to convince everyday Americans to think differently about freedom. In short, they wanted a new idea of liberty—which is why they are often called "neoliberals." But this new liberty was freedom from government regulation for corporations, not freedom to enjoy the fruit of their labor for everyday Americans.

In the internal deliberations among these economists who would redefine liberty for so many Americans, MacLean found that the antigovernment rhetoric that now saturates our political life and its radically different notion of freedom did not come from average people, but from elite extremists in history such as the nineteenth-century pro-slavery senator from South Carolina, John C. Calhoun, who held as many as a hundred people in bondage. Calhoun saw federal power as a menace to the system of slavery and conceptualized "freedom" as the right of slaveholders to make their own decisions about their "property" without intervention or regulation from the government.

Separating Calhoun's notions of freedom and property rights from the brutal institution of human bondage, neoliberal economists and their activist allies began to talk about taxes as "theft" of wages and common goods as "entitlements" that some people did not deserve. "For all its fine phrases," MacLean writes, "what this cause really seeks is a return to oligarchy . . . It would like to reinstate the kind of political economy that prevailed in America at the opening of the twentieth century, when the mass disfranchisement of voters and the legal treatment of labor unions as illegitimate enabled large corporations and wealthy individuals." Again, beware the Trojan horse. This reactionary movement didn't make their case for the concentration of wealth in the hands of a few directly. Instead, they co-opted a basic American value—freedom—and pitted it against the values of equality and the common good. They asked people to take sides, perpetuating the myth that says division is inevitable.

MacLean's work unmasks the story of freedom that has been told to keep poor people from coming together to challenge an unjust economic system, but the myth that says we cannot overcome our divisions could not have been sustained over the past four decades without moral sanction as well. As a pastor, I take this abuse of faith seriously. I am bothered by people who say so much about what God says so little about, and so little about what God says so much about—especially the plight of the poor and rejected in society.

As we've seen, reactionary conservatives who want to hold on to power have claimed the moral high ground since they ruled in the Virginia Assembly that the baptism they offered enslaved Africans did not in any way alter their status as property. Slaveholder religion used Scripture and moral reasoning to justify human bondage and push back against the abolitionists of the early nineteenth century. The white supremacists who overthrew Reconstruction claimed they were "redeeming" the nation. As Princeton University's Kevin Kruse documented in his book *One Nation Under God*, the U.S. Chamber of Commerce surveyed Americans in the 1930s to find who were the most trusted voices to push back against the New Deal. When they learned that preachers had the highest public confidence, they invested in a network of clergy who would proclaim a gospel of individual responsibility and blame poor people rather than exploitative corporate practices for poverty. "With ample funding from major corporations, prominent industrialists, and business lobbies," Kruse writes, "these new evangelists for free enterprise promoted a vision best characterized as 'Christian libertarianism.' " In every era, there have been people who twisted moral and religious values to prop up injustice.

Yet following the gains of the 1960s and '70s, reactionaries within the New Right understood that, in order to build a base for their political and economic goals, they needed to organize white people around their religion rather than their race. A political operative named Paul Weyrich was central to this effort. He recognized that many white churches in the South had used their buildings to establish segregation academies for their white children after the federal government began to mandate the desegregation of public schools in keeping with the Supreme Court's 1954 *Brown v. Board of Education of Topeka* decision. When the Internal Revenue Service said churches could lose their nonprofit status if they used their property to subvert federal law, many white parents were incensed.

Weyrich saw that this anger could be channeled into political organizing, but he knew that segregation was not a winning issue. So he reached out to Jerry Falwell, a preacher in Lynchburg, Virginia, who had served as a local chaplain for people committed to resisting school desegregation and had started a segregation academy for white children in his large Baptist church. Weyrich convinced Falwell that he could mobilize angry white Christians as a "pro-life" movement focused on demonizing the federal government because it allowed abortions, not because it mandated desegregation. As the historians Randall Balmer and Anthea Butler have documented, this is how the Religious Right came to be in American politics. In

a way similar to the neoliberals' effort to pit freedom against
equality, these new culture warriors worked to frame traditional values as opposed to progressive policy. If they could
convince some Christians and Jews that the prophet Isaiah's
challenge of politicians who "legislate evil and rob the poor of
their right" wasn't a traditional value, then they could use their
Sabbath assemblies to reinforce the old myth that says we're
hopelessly divided.

Weyrich was a savvy organizer. He recognized that a majority of Americans did not support the interests of the New Right
and the neoliberal economic theories they wanted to implement through public policy. Still, Weyrich was determined to
organize for minority control of government. "I don't want
everybody to vote. Elections are not won by a majority of the
people," he said at an early meeting of the Religious Right in
1980. "Our leverage in the elections . . . goes up as the voting
populace goes down."

The key to winning, Weyrich understood, was manufacturing divisive debates that would rally his base of conservative
white voters and split up any opposing coalition. He started the
Council for National Policy (CNP) as a coordinating roundtable
where conservative political leaders, heads of religious nonprof-
its, media companies, and donors could coordinate campaigns
to target white faith communities with messaging that would
convince them that the narrow agenda of reactionary conservative politics represents their "traditional values." The CNP
has now invested billions of dollars over the past four decades
in creating a wraparound culture in many rural communities
where the promise of policies that could help everyday people
are demonized as a threat to biblical values. To live within their

echo chamber is to think that so-called conservatives and liberals could never find common cause.

This movement hasn't only targeted white people. When I was a young preacher in Martinsville, Virginia, in the 1980s, a white man in a business suit knocked on my front door at the church parsonage and tried to recruit me for one of the leadership programs that the CNP sponsors. He knew I pastored a historically Black church in town, and he complimented me on a recording of one of my sermons that he said he had listened to. His organization hosted a summer institute for young ministers like me, and he hoped I'd consider attending. They wanted to invest in me, he said, and build a movement that could reclaim America for God. They also didn't want me to say anything about social justice or God's concern for the poor.

Sociologists in America today call people like that man who visited me "white Christian nationalists." They are the heirs of Weyrich's work to both divide and make division feel impossible to overcome. Samuel Perry and Andrew Whitehead have published studies of recent survey results that show how people who identify with white Christian nationalism are more likely to believe it is "too easy to vote" in the United States, believe voter fraud is rampant, think Black Americans are at fault when police use deadly force, and believe American patriots may have to resort to physical violence to save the United States. While not every white Christian nationalist was prepared to storm the Capitol to prevent the nonviolent transfer of power in the United States on January 6, 2021, these are the people who rallied to pray for the insurrectionists when the Justice Department prosecuted them for their crimes. In language he learned from his white evangelical friends who are members of the

CNP, Donald Trump said they were people who "worship God, not government."

When we know this history of neoliberal economics and Christian nationalism, it's clear that the Tea Party and the so-called "populism" of the MAGA movement in American politics did not, in fact, grow out of the "economic anxiety" of hardworking people or the "traditional values" of everyday Americans. These are not home-grown movements tearing at the fabric of our common life. They are, instead, the well-funded propaganda campaigns of elites who have a vested interest in spreading notions of "freedom" and false religion that unite white people in the bondage of an increasingly unequal society—all fueled by the Internet.

It's little wonder that poor and working people are angry in the richest nation in the history of the world. Almost no one in politics will even say their name. When we relaunched the Poor People's Campaign, several political messaging consultants told us that people wouldn't want to identify with a movement that calls them "poor." This didn't make any sense to me. "They know better than anybody that they're poor," I told the consultants.

As I started to travel the country and meet with people who work on factory floors, teach in schools, drive people to appointments, and stock grocery store shelves all week but still can't afford the basic necessities of life, they said it was about time somebody started talking about what's really going on for everyday people in this country. After all, you can't really connect with people where they are if you say you're trying to build a "coalition of those who are just below the middle-class." Folks I met weren't ashamed to be called poor. They were ashamed of a political system that can always tell you who to hate, but can never enact programs that help folks like them get a leg up.

The neoliberal consensus that everyone is going to be okay as long as unemployment is down and the stock market is up has blinded our political leadership to the plight of nearly half of Americans—the people who experience the systemic violence that Coretta Scott King named at the Poor People's Campaign's Solidarity Day in 1968. "Even contempt for poverty is violence," she said. I've learned that tens of millions of Americans feel the violence of that contempt in their aching bones.

With no one to fight for the growing numbers of poor people, the myth that says we can't overcome our divisions became widely accepted as true. Without the prospect of any real alternative to the status quo, more and more Americans increasingly came to distrust government, think private enterprise was more efficient, and believe that they knew best what to do with their hard-earned money. What's more, many were told that this was God's plan. But, as I said, poor people are not stupid. They know they've been lied to by politicians, which is why many of them opted out of the political process all together. If they were on their own, they figured taking care of themselves and their loved ones should be their priority.

I knew as we relaunched the Poor People's Campaign in 2018 that, if we could expose the myth that says it's not possible to come together, then the people who know the real impact of poverty become the base we need for a mass movement that can fundamentally change American politics. Every Republican and Democrat political consultant knows that control of the White House and Congress depends on a turnout race between bases that are roughly the same size. Electoral campaigns in this context are constantly about identifying hot-button issues that will excite each party's base and exploit the vulnerabilities of the other party's candidate. Both sides have an incredible amount of data about voters in every district of the country, so American politics is often locked into a pattern where the pendulum can only swing so far in one direction or the other.

In almost every American election, though, the block of eligible voters who *choose not to vote* is larger than the number of voters who turn out for either party's candidate. Because we knew that eligible, inactive voters are overwhelmingly poor people who can see that the way things are isn't working for them, we also knew that if we could build a movement that both informed poor people about their potential power and gave them a platform to shape the conversation about what matters in public life, then a moral fusion coalition of poor people and their allies could reconstruct America. The key was to get past the wedge issues that people so often end up fighting about and get this essential information directly to the people. We had to expose the myth that says we can't overcome our divisions.

I'll never forget the day we went to Harlan County, Kentucky, one of the poorest counties in Eastern Kentucky, as we were relaunching the Poor People's Campaign. Harlan County is south of Martin County, where President Lyndon Johnson went to launch the War on Poverty in 1964. These hills hadn't seen a presidential visit before that day, when Marine One came over a hill and landed in an open field, and they haven't seen one since. The myth of freedom that neoliberals crafted in their think tanks has shaped local culture here from the Christian libertarianism that's preached on gospel radio stations to the antigovernment ads that senators Rand Paul and Mitch McConnell run every reelection season. Some people told us we were crazy to go up there, but Harlan County was just the kind of place where we wanted to test our campaign's message.

As we drove in, I noticed how the railroad tracks hugged the sides of the hills, which were dotted with little clapboard houses that seemed to hang off the side of the mountain. The hollowed-out towns we passed through looked like they'd seen their prime when I was a child. The buildings that weren't shuttered were faded. We arrived at an old school building and were greeted by Black and white miners who'd asked to meet with us. I sat down with them and told them about my grandfather on my momma's side, who'd been a coal miner over in West Virginia. Then I asked them to tell me what was going on in their community. One of the miners said, "They sell us out."

I said, "What do you mean by that?"

He started to tell me about how politicians had come up there talking about how gay people were supposedly threatening their values, but then they went to D.C. and allowed multinational corporations to come in and take over the mining operations without doing anything to protect the miners' pensions or their healthcare or the mountains they called home. Now those companies were blowing the tops off of mountains in order to get the coal without having to pay people to go down into the earth to get it. And they weren't doing anything to take care of the people who'd worked in those mines for years and were now sick with black lung and other illnesses.

That wasn't the worst of it, though. One of the old miners said, "If you go back in them woods there, you'll find a whole camp full of young people. They got kicked out of their homes 'cause of all this talk about the 'homosexual agenda' and how it was going to destroy our community. Well, some people believed it, and they kicked their kids out when they told 'em they were gay. Now them kids are strung out on drugs, and these assholes who told us our kids were going to destroy the community have handed it over to companies that are willing to blow up the mountain just to make money."

Those miners could see how the culture wars that kept the old myth of inevitable division alive were tearing their community apart. They were as politically astute as any political strategist I ever met. They could see what was happening, and they wanted to help us organize a moral fusion coalition to stand against it. We all drove over to a church in the little town where we were going to have lunch with people who'd come to do a training in moral fusion organizing. A whole busload of folks from Louisville had ridden out to learn who their allies might be in Eastern Kentucky. When I walked into the room in this tiny little town, it was packed to the rafters with people ready to hear how we might work together to achieve something better than the poverty they knew.

Our team at Repairers of the Breach had created a set of slides to help folks see how issues that impact poor communities interlock in U.S. politics. On the first slide, a map of the United States highlights areas with the highest levels of poverty, linking Appalachia with large stretches of the South and the Midwest. On a second slide, we overlaid states that have passed voter suppression measures since 2010. The geographic areas matched almost precisely. Then, on subsequent slides, we highlighted the states that have passed antiabortion or anti-LGBTQ legislation to fuel the "culture war" that has been pushed by the Southern Strategy. With each overlay, the same areas of the country kept getting highlighted. When we showed the states that refused to expand Medicaid under the Affordable Care Act, the states matched up again. Then, finally, we overlaid a map showing the highest concentration of white evangelical Protestants. There it was again—the same pattern.

The data demonstrated what the old miners knew from experience. The politicians who pushed culture war wedge issues and freedom from government had sold their message as "traditional values" to communities where a majority of the electorate was made up of white Christians. The places represented by these politicians were some of the poorest in the nation.

When I'd finished going over the slides, a man sitting toward the back of the church said, "Show me those slides again, Reverend." I clicked back through them quickly, naming the interlocking issues as they piled up on top of communities like the one where we were sitting.

"Well, I'll be damned," the man said after I'd finished going through the slides again. "They've been playing us against one another." This fellow told me he was a member of the McCoy family, of the infamous Hatfield and McCoy family feud in Eastern Kentucky and West Virginia. The heir of a family divided against its neighbors since the Civil War, he was moved by a story that explained in simple terms how the identity he and his people had been offered generation after generation was based on a myth that serves elite interests far removed from the hill country that he loves.

His testimony that day became a sign to me: a real McCoy had shown up to bear witness that Americans who've been pitted against one another by an endless regurgitation of this nation's old myths are hungry for a better story to tell them who they are. I didn't know how long it would take, but I knew that day as I watched the faces in the congregation that a room full of white people in Harlan County were going home to tell their families and neighbors that, together with their Black and brown neighbors, they can become something better. Maybe this was more than a campaign to change the conversation about political possibilities in the next election. Maybe we were caught up in a movement to become the nation we were meant to be.

PART III

Reconstructing Democracy

Rev Barber listens at a community meeting
in Corbin, Kentucky.

Chapter 7

FACING WHITE
POVERTY'S WOUNDS

L EAVING MY HOUSE IN GOLDSBORO, NORTH CAR-
olina, in October 2019, I drove through the hills of the
Blue Ridge Mountains, painted deep rust, bright orange, and
golden by autumn's changing leaves, to Corbin, Kentucky. An
old railroad stop in coal country, Corbin had been a social and
economic hub for folks who live in the hollers of Eastern Kentucky for decades. It's where one of Kentucky's most famous
sons—Colonel Sanders—got his start frying chicken. People
who've lived here for generations think of Corbin as an all-
white town, but it was not always so. Like Mitchell County,
North Carolina, Corbin recruited Black men to work on the
railroad in the early twentieth century. But the old myth that
tells people who think of themselves as white to see Black people as a threat did its work here. In 1919, after two Black railroad workers were accused of robbing a white man in town, a
mob formed and went door-to-door through Corbin, forcing
terrified Black people to board the next train out of town. To
survive, Black people left everything they had worked for and
fled for their lives. This was how Corbin, Kentucky, became an
all-white town. Here, as in so many places, the violence of our
history is buried beneath the veneer of everyday life.

The hidden violence that courses through a place like Corbin doesn't only impact the Black families who lost everything. It also lives on in the false identity that the old myths offer white people. As the Scriptures say, the sins of the fathers are visited upon their children, even to the third and fourth generations. I saw what that looks like in Corbin. At an event to remember the hundredth anniversary of this forgotten history, I met Lakin, a young white woman who wore a University of Eastern Kentucky T-shirt and had the flushed cheeks of someone who was sharing the most difficult struggles of her life with other people for the first time. In a little church where Black and white people had gathered to tell the truth about their history and talk about organizing for a better future for all people in Kentucky, Lakin shared stories about the fear of Black people and immigrants that had been commonplace in her family and school when she was growing up. She talked about how she admired her parents for the ways they worked hard to provide for her and her siblings, even when good work was hard to find and unpaid bills piled up like dirty laundry. When Lakin started to come to terms with the fact that she was queer, she realized that the people in her life said the same kinds of things about her and her sexuality that they said about Black people and immigrants.

"It was all rooted in fear," she told the folks gathered in the church that day, recalling how kids in her community were sent on a "Journey Through Hell" hayride each autumn, where scenes of eternal damnation were performed as public spectacles, as if from a medieval passion play. Churches promoted the event to "get people saved," but it occurred to Lakin that the hayride demanded young people conform to the social norms of white culture, all in God's name.

When Lakin's dad lost his construction job, his recreational drug use became such a debilitating addiction that he and the family were deeply ashamed. Her parents separated, and when she and her siblings stayed with her dad, they had to collect rainwater and boil it on a wood-fired stove before they could drink it. Lakin recalled that her mom, who worked overtime to make up for the missing child support, would often wait until late at night, when no one else was at the local grocery store, to shop with the food stamps that subsidized her low wages. But when Lakin came out, she was shunned by her family. She had to live in her car for stints as a young adult while she worked three minimum-wage jobs to pay her way through college. All the while, she wrestled with the basic contradiction that her parents were both her biggest heroes and loved ones whose fears had turned them against her.

"I'm sick of living in fear—and letting that silence me," Lakin told the group gathered on the hundredth anniversary of the expulsion of Black folks from Corbin. I watched the tears well up in her eyes when she couldn't find the words to say what it all meant to her, and I sensed that we were on holy ground. In a sacred place, where people gather every Sunday to worship God, a young white woman's honesty had exposed the reality that is too often hidden in American public life. The shame she described was familiar to me: I'd felt it when I first saw those images of Black mothers in welfare lines as a child. As a pastor, I have seen it when people faced eviction or had to ask the church for money because, despite working multiple jobs to make ends meet, they couldn't fix the car and pay the light bill that month.

Black folks know what it means to bear the double-bind of poverty—unable to make ends meet, and at the same time, being blamed for one's predicament, as if it's your fault. When you know that the stories bandied about that stigmatize your existence are a lie, though, you develop spiritual and cultural resources to resist them. Every Sunday for forty years, I've preached in the gospel tradition that tells people to stand up straight and know that they are beloved children of God, even when they know they must walk out the doors of the church into a world where a cruel concentration of lies tell them they're worthless. Many white people don't have this kind of restorative gospel. Too often, even the sermon they hear on Sunday morning has been turned against them—twisted to justify the very social order that is making their lives unlivable.

When Lakin, raised in the hills of Eastern Kentucky, confessed the confusion of being white and poor, I knew she was articulating something unique about white poverty: *it is a curse that people are too often damned to bear alone.*

The sad reality of our shared life in this country is that the poverty and financial vulnerability that isolates millions of white people is the experience of *all* Americans who lack financial security. Poverty isn't that rare glitch in the current U.S. economy. Poverty is a feature of our economy's design. The extreme wealth that a smaller and smaller minority enjoys depends on the isolation of people like Lakin and her family. It's one thing to note, as Nancy MacLean and other historians have, that our common lives since the mid-twentieth century have trended toward growing inequality and greater isolation, but appreciating this history is not the same as knowing Lakin. White people who've both faced the daily realities of poverty and wrestled with the fears that our old myths offer as an answer to their predicament have helped me understand how the policy decisions that have led us here interlock, just as the experiences of injustice increasingly intersect. To know the way out of the mess we're in, we must learn from the experience of people like Lakin.

When we face white poverty and its effects, we see a painful reality that has too often been hidden from our public discourse. The daily, ongoing traumatic stress that all poor people face always lands on particular people in specific places. Someone like Lakin has been directly impacted by corporate lobbyists' unceasing efforts to keep wages low while productivity has increased and corporate profits have soared. All the while, she has also been represented by so-called "conservative" politicians who've resisted investment in healthcare, affordable housing, and education—the real costs of living that kept Lakin sleeping in her car, even when she was "doing everything right," according to the twisted narratives that try to blame poor people for their poverty. Those same political leaders—along with their religious allies and media partners—divert attention from the problems facing everyday people by claiming that immigrants or people who are queer or women who choose not to have a baby are the real enemies. "It is all rooted in fear," Lakin observed when the hatred that had been directed at other people was turned on her. The fear is what isolated her from the very neighbors who would eventually offer the support and community she needed to survive. And the fear was what sepa-rated her from her parents—her heroes who had fought so hard to make her life and their own bearable.

At that little church in Corbin, when she could not summon the words to explain why she felt so much pain inside of her, Lakin fell into the embrace of me and my sister Liz from the Poor People's Campaign.

"I'm sorry, I'm sorry," Lakin muttered, her head buried in my shoulder.

"It's alright, go ahead and cry," I told her. And while she let the tears flow, I turned to the room full of folks who'd just witnessed her vulnerability. "We need to thank our sister for inviting us into a sacred space," I told them. "I hope each of us can take a minute to grieve the ways we've been hurt by the lies that are used to divide us."

It's important to remember that white folks hurt like every other human being. Their stomachs growl like everyone else's when they are hungry; their bones ache when they are sick; their muscles tense and tremble when they are left out in the cold without shelter. This, I've learned, is the source of solidar-ity among poor people: if you can't pay your light bill, we're all Black in the dark.

When I did my doctoral work at Drew University in pastoral theology and public policy, I took a course in forensic psychol-ogy. I'd seen depictions of forensic labs on detective shows and I had watched the way evidence shapes a murder investigation in criminal cases that were reported in the news, but I'd never met a forensic psychologist. Every week in class, we listened to case studies. I had the chance to learn from people who spend their lives trying to understand crimes after the fact, with only the evidence that remains. I'll never forget what one of the lecturers said to us: "You have to begin with the wound, because wounds speak."

A knife wound in the gut, for instance, suggests intimacy to a forensic psychologist. It raises the question, who was close to the victim, and who might have had reason to be angry with them? When people are honest about the ways they've been hurt, their wounds often tell the story of the people and experiences that have shaped their lives, for good and for ill. If this is true for the care of souls, it is equally true for our care of society. When we pay attention to the wounds of policy violence, the wounds speak. They not only tell us how we got here. When we are willing to listen, they can also help us make the necessary connections between people who are hurting and the public policies that could make a real difference in their lives.

When we listen to the often hidden wounds of white poverty, they point us toward a reality that touches every race and region of this nation. To face white poverty's wounds is not to dismiss race. I abhor America's original sin of racism, but by interrupting the ways race isolates us, I want to flip the conversation we usually have about poverty on its head. I want to examine the evidence of white poverty's violence so we can see through the cracks in a broken system that have been covered up and painted over for far too long.

Early on in our organizing with the Poor People's Campaign, I got an invitation to visit Binghamton, New York, and meet with folks who'd begun organizing there. While I've been in and out of New York City much of my adult life, I had always wanted to visit "upstate." Growing up, I heard stories about enslaved people who got away to the North. I always imagined upstate New York as a land of promise and freedom. I wanted to go to Rochester and walk the streets where Frederick Douglass lived and inhale the free air that Harriet Tubman breathed before she risked her life to go back and bring others out of bondage. When the call came to visit Binghamton, I was eager to go. My first thought was that this would be a chance to reflect on how the past can inspire us to work for freedom and justice in the present.

What I saw as I drove into town was a faded city not unlike those towns in Eastern Kentucky whose glory days seem to be in the rearview mirror. Big factory buildings that used to employ hundreds of people sat vacant. Storefronts were shuttered, leaving streets that used to bustle with people quiet and marked by potholes. Homes that working families built in the mid-twentieth century had been passed down to the generation that grew up in them, but it looked like most folks with the resources to keep the places up had moved on. The houses that were still inhabited were in sore need of repair.

Our Poor People's Campaign event met in an old church downtown with red carpet, large arched doorways, and a huge oil painting of Jesus under the dome at the front of the sanctuary. The place had been built to hold a crowd, but it hadn't seen one this size in some time. Though we made sure the people sharing up front were Black and white to represent the fusion coalition we were building, almost everyone I could see who filled the pews all the way to the back was white.

Everything suddenly started tumbling out. As folks shared their stories, some remembered the "Square Deal" of good factory jobs in a company town where bosses had seen the benefit of making sure everyone had access to healthcare, education, and recreation. Back in the day, Binghamton was the shoe capital of the country. After the factories closed their doors, though, the jobs left and the government did nothing to step in and meet basic needs. A middle-aged white woman said she had grown up in the years when the local economy was being hollowed out. She stood at the microphone and shared her earliest memory of her mother putting her in foster care because she couldn't afford to take care of her anymore. "I remember the little doll she gave me. It had blond hair and a blue dress, and it came with a little washcloth and a fake bar of soap." At two years old, she had a doll that looked like her with everything it needed to stay pretty and clean. Yet her family had been ripped apart by poverty. "Everyone I know is poor," she told the folks gathered in the church that evening.

Determined unlike her mother to keep her own children with her, this woman dropped out of college and took a minimum-wage job while she was still a teenager. She had in the end raised four children, but at times when she went months without any income, she recalled having to scavenge in dumpsters for food to feed them. "I was recently diagnosed with PTSD," she told us, "but I'm glad to be part of a community that recognizes my expertise as someone with a lived experience of poverty."

I was hit between the eyes by the reality of America's post-industrial economy, where millions of people suffer, even in so-called liberal states where politicians claim to stand with poor and working people. The data tell us poverty is worst in places where antigovernment, reactionary conservatives control local and state government, but the wounds of poverty among mostly white people in a place like Binghamton make something else clear: we have a bipartisan consensus in this country that corporate freedom matters more than the lives of everyday American people.

Early in 2023, a research team led by Dr. David Brady of the University of California, Riverside published a report that quantified this shocking wound of our common life. Poverty, they found, is the fourth leading cause of death in America—more deadly than obesity or diabetes, both of which are exacerbated by poverty, and more deadly than firearms. Brady said he decided to run the numbers after witnessing the outcry against gun deaths and a public conversation about what policies could reduce them. While there is a Second Amendment that protects the right of Americans to bear arms, there is no amendment to protect us from poverty. If far more people are dying from poverty than from guns, why aren't there more conversations about what could reduce it?

Drawing on data from a longitudinal study of people from communities across the country, Brady and his team found that, beginning around age 40, the life expectancy of people who are currently poor begins to diverge dramatically from that of their neighbors who are not. For those who are poor year after year, the gap is even wider. From the demographics of poverty across the country, we know this means Black, brown, and Native communities are disproportionately impacted. But if 800 people are dying each day from poverty in America, roughly half of those casualties are white.

As we saw during the COVID-19 pandemic, we treat it as a public health emergency when hundreds of people are dying every day from a pathogen. We invest major resources in developing vaccines and treatments; we dramatically alter the regular patterns of our daily life; and we rally as communities to take care of people who are vulnerable. We do this because we value our own lives and the lives of our neighbors. This is why Americans have been able to make major investments as well as cultural and policy changes to end child labor practices, provide Social Security and Medicare to elders, combat lung cancer, and reduce deaths from automobile accidents. If we know that poverty is killing more people than automobile accidents, strokes, or drug overdoses, why can't we get everyone on board for a "moonshot" to end poverty? Why don't we have a "Surgeon General's Warning" on low-wage jobs?

When we listen to the wounds of white poverty, they reveal something about the perpetrators of this particular form of violence. The moral malady of people who are benefiting from the economic policies that kill poor people every day is that they do not understand themselves to be like the people who are dying. A forensic psychologist would tell us that the wounds I witnessed in Binghamton were neither inflicted in passion nor created by an act of self-defense; they are more like the wound suffered by a pedestrian struck by a drunk driver who doesn't remember the next morning that he ran over another human being. Many Americans have accustomed themselves to unnecessary death because they are so drunk on the promise of profit and progress that they do not even see the people who are being crushed. White poverty's wounds tell us that, if we are going to reconstruct American democracy, we must address this crisis of conscience.

Our religious traditions offer resources for this task of reclaiming our moral center. Repeatedly, the prophets say, "Seek good and not evil, and you will live." But when leadership is corrupt and policies are crushing the poor and the vulnerable, the prophets always say to the nation, "Your choices are killing you. Your leadership is killing your people and your possibilities. And if you desire to be the nation God would have you be, seek good, not evil, and live." America is made up of many religious traditions, but all of them challenge the greed that has been normalized in an economy that puts profit over people.

White poverty's wounds call us to tell the truth about an economic system that is killing us. I remember five white women I met in West Virginia who work low-wage jobs to keep a roof over their heads and put food on their tables. On Tuesdays, these women set up a little folding table on the roadside to sell tacos to passers-by. The money they made went into a shared fund to buy feminine care products for themselves and other women in the community who could not afford these basic necessities of life, even though many of them are working two and three jobs.

Like the vast majority of poor people, these women are the so-called "working poor." But this way of naming people in their situation was developed by the forces that want to pit poor people against one another by suggesting that some, who are working, deserve public support, while others do not. A study in 2017 found that only 3 percent of working-age adults were out of the labor market for unknown reasons. Most poor people are working—some offering unpaid care to family members, others getting paid less than a living wage by corporations that consistently get government handouts in the form of tax breaks, bailouts, and even the government assistance that subsidizes their workers through food stamps and Medicaid. Often, it's all of the above—plus side hustles like Taco Tuesdays just to make ends meet. Rather than call them the "working poor," we should call them the victims of poverty wages.

When we face white poverty's wounds, they show us how allowing employers to pay their workers less than a living wage is a policy choice that affects all of us. And it does not have to be this way. In 1933, Frances Perkins, a no-nonsense and deeply faithful woman, became America's first female labor secretary. She was moved by the Social Gospel, a theology that emphasizes the demand for justice in the teachings of Jesus, and her own examination of poverty's wounds to press President Franklin Delano Roosevelt to advocate for a federal minimum wage. After signing the legislation that made this piece of the New Deal a reality, Roosevelt said, "No business which depends for its existence on paying less than living wages to its workers has any right to continue in this country." The "middle class" that so many politicians on both sides of the aisle like to talk about today was not created by the invisible hand of an unchecked free market. It was the product of policy decisions, including a federal minimum wage.

Because many nonwhite workers were excluded from the economic uplift of the New Deal, A. Philip Randolph, who founded the first labor union for Black workers in the United States, made certain that the agenda for the 1963 March on Washington, which he helped organize, included union rights and a living wage of $2 an hour for all Americans. Today, when we remember the March on Washington, most Americans think about Martin Luther King Jr.'s dream of a society where people would be judged not by the "color of their skin, but the content of their character." But the organizers originally billed it as a march for "Jobs and Freedom." If the $2 an hour minimum wage they demanded then were indexed for inflation, it would be almost $17 an hour today.

Despite a nearly 50-percent cumulative price increase since Congress last raised the minimum wage in 2009, the floor for wages in the United States is still $7.25 an hour in 2023. And for tipped workers, it's $2.16, allowing employers to pass even more of the cost of labor on to their customers. I've stood with service workers in the Fight for $15 since they launched their campaign to raise the minimum wage in 2013, and I have heard politicians repeat the arguments against them: higher wages will increase unemployment because companies will have to cut costs by cutting jobs, they say. Low-wage workers know this is not an economic argument based on real-world data.

In 1992, when New Jersey raised its minimum wage and neighboring Pennsylvania did not, Princeton University's David Card and Alan Krueger recognized the opportunity to test the argument against raising wages. They surveyed 410 fast-food-restaurant workers in both states before and after the minimum wage increase and found that fast-food jobs didn't disappear in New Jersey when the minimum wage went up. "Our empirical findings challenge the prediction that a rise in the minimum reduces employment," Card and Krueger concluded. Professor Card went on to share the Nobel Prize in economics in 2021 for his research that dispels the myth that raising wages necessarily costs jobs.

Yet white poverty's wounds scream to us that low wages continue to threaten the lives of millions of Americans. Thousands of years ago, the biblical prophet Jeremiah wrote, "Woe to him who builds his palace by unrighteousness, his upper rooms by injustice, making his own people work for nothing, not paying them for their labor." When the ancients called prophets "seers," they didn't mean that they had magical powers to look into a crystal ball and foretell the details of a future none of us can know. Instead, they meant that seers can see the patterns of our shared life and know where our choices are leading us. When politicians believe the lies that justify poverty wages, they make decisions that undermine all of us—including themselves. Poverty isn't only deadly for the poor. It is killing the promises of democracy.

Still, the prophet's "woe" isn't a curse in the sense that it damns anyone's possibility to do justice and love mercy. As long as we can still hear the prophets' warnings, there's time for us to change course. The prophet's woe is more like a "wrong way" sign posted on the exit ramp of a highway. If we continue to make people work for nothing, Jeremiah declares, we are headed for destruction. When we undercut workers, we weaken the very foundation of our common life.

White poverty's wounds don't only reveal how people with resources have been allowed to run roughshod over folks who do the essential work that keeps our society running. They also tell us, if we're willing to listen, how the same people who are enriched by low-wage labor also try to silence the voices of the neighbors they are abusing—people like Stanley Sturgill. I met Stanley at a rally outside the statehouse in Frankfort, Kentucky, in the spring of 2018. A stocky man with a short-cut gray beard, Stanley became a coal miner when it was the best union job available in his hometown of Lynch, Kentucky. He worked 41 years in the coal mines underneath Black Mountain, the highest peak in Eastern Kentucky, but over the course of Stanley's career, unions in America were decimated by the same forces in our public life that worked to keep wages down.

Throughout the 1950s and '60s, when men like Stanley were growing up, nearly a third of all U.S. workers were union members. With the strength of their unions, those workers were able to negotiate not only decent wages, but also healthcare and retirement plans that would allow them and their families a level of economic security that's unimaginable for half of Americans today. But in pursuit of greater profits for themselves and their investors, the same corporate interests that pushed to keep wages down also undermined workers by attacking unions. They pushed so-called "right to work" legislations in statehouses, establishing legal barriers to union organizing, and funded propaganda campaigns against the unions that generations of workers had built to protect themselves and future generations from corporate greed. Today, only 10 percent of American workers are members of a union, down from 35 percent in the 1950s.

No single demographic has suffered more from the decline in union membership than white men without a college degree. Between 1979 and 2017—roughly the decades Stanley worked in Kentucky's coal mines—white men like him saw their earnings decrease by 13 percent. Economists Anne Case and Angus Deaton have connected this decline in economic well-being with an increase in morbidity among the same demographic—a phenomenon they name "deaths of despair." Yes, poverty kills because sick people can't access healthcare and the compounded stress of not knowing how you're going to pay your bills takes its toll on the body. There is also a psychological impact when people lose their collective means of having their voices heard.

The spike in liver disease, drug overdose, and suicide that Case and Deaton identify among white men who have lost the shared power of unions is another wound of white poverty. At the same time that the old myths told these men they were responsible for pulling themselves up by their bootstraps, many poor white people lost the basic infrastructure that kept them in a regular supply of boots. Thus, many men in Stanley's situation found themselves barefoot and alone, feeling like they were to blame for the pain that they and their families were experiencing. Like Lakin's dad, some turned to drugs for an escape. Or, as a farmer's wife told me when I visited her community in Kansas, some men tried to make their suicide look like a farming accident so their families could collect enough to survive off their life insurance policies.

When we listen to these wounds of white poverty, they whisper the connections between low wages and the loss of unions—between poverty that kills the body and, at the same time, threatens to kill our democracy. The link, I've come to realize, is the way each person's voice is tied to their basic dignity. In my faith tradition, we understand humans to be created in the image of God—every life a reflection of the One who creates and sustains life. Human dignity and the inherent value of life that is rooted in our creation story is also reflected in God's gift of voice to humans. Of all the creatures, God invites the human to speak the names of the other animals. God speaks life into being in the Genesis story. Then God gives us a voice to speak. Indeed, the sign that things have gone awry in the Bible's creation story is the lonely silence when God calls and the humans do not respond. It is a terrible thing for people to lose their voice.

My rabbi friends taught me that the Hebrew word for voice in the ancient creation story—*kol*—is the same word they use for "vote" in modern Hebrew. While people may join their voices together in unions or political parties, the basic voice each citizen over eighteen years of age is supposed to have in America's democracy is their vote. No matter where you live or what your net worth is, your voice is your vote in our system of government. When we face white poverty's wounds, they reveal an essential connection between the loss of living wages and the attack on voting rights in this country.

Of course, many people's voices were excluded from public life from the beginning of America's democratic experiment. Women, Native Americans, enslaved people, and those who did not own land were excluded from voting by the same framers who declared that all people are created equal. Still, the promise of equal access to the franchise has inspired movements that have amended the Constitution to expand access to the ballot. The Fifteenth Amendment guaranteed voting rights to the formerly enslaved after the Civil War. The Nineteenth Amendment expanded voting rights to women in 1920. Forty-four years later, the United States ratified the Twenty-Fourth Amendment to the Constitution, eliminating poll taxes that had been used across the South to abridge access to the ballot. Less than a decade after that, the Twenty-Sixth Amendment lowered the voting age from 21 to 18. With each of these steps, more voices were included in American public life.

In a reaction against this expansion of democracy, the same

forces that have worked to keep wages low and curtail the influence of unions have also worked to limit access to the ballot for poor people. Since the Supreme Court's 2013 decision in *Shelby County v. Holder*, the 1965 Voting Rights Act, which provided protections against voter suppression, especially in places with a history of exclusion, has been stripped of its power to check state legislatures where a majority wants to pass election law changes that make it more difficult for people to vote. So-called "election integrity" measures have been introduced in states with long histories of voter suppression, using the contemporary tools of voter roll purges or voter ID requirements to narrow the voting pool and reduce the potential power of a multiethnic voting coalition.

I call this reality James Crow, Esquire—the result of Jim Crow's son going to law school and coming back to undermine democracy through more sophisticated means. Is it still racist? Yes. But as we've seen, racism is never just about limiting the rights of Black people. Racist voter suppression may target Black people, but it hurts most of us. If we're going to beat James Crow, we have to connect all the people who are impacted by these attacks. Jim Crow was brought down by a moral fusion movement during America's Second Reconstruction in the 1960s, but his son went to law school and came back to state legislatures in a business suit. His data analysis and legal maneuvers are more sophisticated than the old Jim Crow's, but James Crow, Esquire's goal is the same: minority rule to preserve an unequal society while giving lip service to democracy.

At the same time that the real value of earnings for poor and low-wage workers has gone down in the United States, the voices of poor people in public life have been diminished.

Rolling back voter access, purging voting rolls, requiring strict forms of voter ID, and gerrymandering districts so that reactionary conservatives can win a majority of the seats without getting a majority of the votes are all tools of James Crow, Esquire. These practices have been deemed racially discriminatory by federal courts because they disproportionately harm Black voters and voters of color. But in raw numbers, more poor white people are impacted by voter suppression than Black or Latino voters. This, too, is a wound that white poverty has left on our body politic.

In 2013, I was very aware of these increased voter restrictions at the time as I was president of the North Carolina NAACP. We sued the North Carolina governor in federal court to stop an omnibus voter suppression bill that bundled dozens of voter suppression measures in one piece of legislation. We developed a legal strategy that recognized how racist voter suppression harms a wide range of people. Rather than simply bringing suit as a civil rights organization representing African Americans who would be harmed by the law, the North Carolina NAACP joined the League of Women Voters, students, congregations and others who had standing before the court because they, too, would be impacted by the proposed changes.

Mother Rosanell Eaton, a stately Black elder who'd beaten Jim Crow in her twenties only to face disenfranchisement by a voter ID requirement in her eighties, was our lead plaintiff on the case, but she wasn't alone. Young people who would not be allowed to vote with a student ID could be turned away at the polls. Cuts to early voting threatened access to the ballot for low-wage workers who could not set their own schedules to get to their polling place on a Tuesday, when they might be sent to work a job two counties away. Plaintiffs who represented these voters also joined the case.

When the court found that the law targeted African Americans with "almost surgical precision," it was not just a victory for Black voters in North Carolina. It also meant continued access for many white voters who would have lost access to early voting or could have been turned away for lack of an approved ID. In raw numbers, no demographic would have been more severely impacted than poor white voters. They're not only the single largest group of citizens who need expanded access to get to the polls. They're also the single largest demographic that stands to benefit from the policies that could be passed if a new governing majority could enact living wages, union protections, universal access to healthcare, and other policies that the vast majority of Americans say they want.

Whether or not they vote for politicians who champion these policies, poor white people benefit from expansions of democracy that lead to more progressive policies. This was true of both the First and Second Reconstruction. Stanford University's Gavin Wright used empirical evidence from the South after the Civil Rights movement to substantiate this claim, which is often disputed by those who continue to believe the old myths that feed racial division. If Black people win, white people lose, they say. As we've seen, the fear of Black people exercising political power has been a main driver of the old myths, from the stories that inspired lynchings after the Civil War to the hysteria over Black and white children sitting next to one another in school. Whenever Black people stand to gain power in America's democracy, the old myths tell white people that it's a threat to property values, their "hard-earned" money, or their very way of life.

Wright found that the numbers don't bear this out, though. Following the Voting Rights Act of 1965, the median income for Black people in the South increased steadily. But wages for white people, which were already considerably higher, increased *at the same rate.* When barriers to voting were removed, people elected leaders who passed policies that improved living conditions for everyone. The inverse of this is also true, though: when votes are suppressed, people who support regressive policies get elected.

This silencing of poor people's voices at the ballot box is directly connected to changes in voting law, as we demonstrated in federal court. This suppression also happens, though, as a by-product of poor people's isolation. Amy Melissa Widestrom, for her PhD dissertation at Syracuse University, analyzed data on the socioeconomic changes in neighborhoods over the past half century and compared that information with voter turnout data from particular neighborhoods. She found that, even apart from changes in voting laws, the more poor people are segregated in places with other poor people, the less they participate in local and national elections. "This understudied and complex dynamic of increasing economic segregation and declining political participation and mobilization suggests a vicious cycle of political behavior and public policy," she wrote, "one in which the capacity of low-income Americans to hold elected representatives accountable and to shape the policy agenda may be severely diminished." Widestrom looked at the numbers and found what poor people all across this nation have helped me to see. We're not only a nation plagued by poverty. We have become an impoverished democracy.

If we listen to white poverty's wounds, they tell us that silencing the voices of people who are hurting is detrimental to social health for all of us. I know from experience that the old myths hide the impact of America's exceptional inequality from many of us by hiding white poverty. When I first asked researchers who were helping us with the Poor People's Campaign to disaggregate the numbers of poor Americans by race, they were hesitant. Many of them good white liberals, they were always careful to emphasize the disproportionate impact of poverty on Black, Hispanic, Asian, and Native American communities. "If we disaggregate the numbers," one of them said to me, "they'll show that the largest group of poor and low-income Americans are white people."

"And that's the point," I said. The old myths are tricky, and they can catch any of us in their trap. Yes, it's racist to pass policies that we know will harm Black people. At the same time, it is also racist to *ignore* the ways those same policies hurt poor white people—because racism's myths are designed to keep Black and white people segregated so they cannot come together to transform a system that doesn't serve most of us. If we're going to be anti-racist and reconstruct an America for all of us, we can't ignore this reality. We have to face the facts that emerge when we pay attention to white poverty's wounds and learn to make the connections between living wages, union rights, and voting rights.

Chapter 8

POOR PEOPLE ARE THE
NEW SWING VOTERS

I HAVE SPENT ENOUGH TIME WITH POOR WHITE folks in America to know that the people themselves are not the problem. Whenever someone asks, "Is it race or is it class?," my answer is, "Yes, it is."

When I go to the hollers of Eastern Kentucky or a small town in Kansas, I never shy away from talking about race. I am a Black man who knows that racism is America's original sin.

"But doesn't all that talk about slavery and Jim Crow just keep us stuck in the divisions of the past?" some ask.

"Only if we misunderstand the past," I say.

Yes, America's history is rife with violence that has denigrated Black people and set our white neighbors against us. When we tell the truth about the movements that successfully challenged slavery and Jim Crow, though, we know that they were multiracial fusion movements. This is why we can't ignore race. Poor white people in America today can learn from the long struggle for racial justice—just as the folks up in Mitchell County chose to learn from the NAACP and the community in Belhaven followed Mamie Till's example to challenge the violence of unnecessary death in their community. Moral fusion means always understanding the role race plays in public life.

When I talk about race, I insist on talking about it along with an analysis that helps folks understand how all poor people suffer when we're pitted against one another.

"But if you focus on the class struggle that poor Black people share with poor white people," others ask, "doesn't that diminish the particular suffering Black people experience in a white supremacist society?"

"Only if we allow our suffering to define who we are."

Race *has* shaped a world where people suffer differently, and we must never diminish the struggle that anyone faces because of the particular ways this world's injustices have piled up on them. Still, no one ever wins a competition of trying to prove that their pain hurts worse than someone else's. When we are honest, we have to acknowledge that injustice may touch us in different ways, but it has a universal effect of choking the life out of our dreams and possibilities. There is a leveling effect to the graveyard, where all who've been beaten up by this world's evils are equally dead.

In the Bible, God tells the prophet Ezekiel to warn the people that there is "a conspiracy of her princes within her like a roaring lion tearing its prey." Political leaders in Ezekiel's day cared more about power than they did about the people who were crushed by their policy violence. The data of Ezekiel's day made this clear, but God called Ezekiel to try to articulate the severity of the situation. So the prophet looked to the natural world and compared the political leadership first to a roaring lion, and later to ravenous wolves. "They shed blood and kill people to make unjust gain," Ezekiel said plainly. He also pointed out that religion had been distorted to prop up this extremism. "Her prophets whitewash these deeds for them. . . . They say, 'This is what the Sovereign LORD says,'—when the LORD has not spoken."

When the powerful collude with immoral leaders to justify policy violence, people are consumed. This is what white poverty's wounds reveal, and it's what the ancient prophet saw. Ezekiel testified that God led him to a valley of dry bones—a graveyard where the dead were not even given the dignity of a proper burial. In a striking vision, the prophet challenges us to face the reality of an economic system that is choking the life out of people: bones from which the flesh has been consumed by wild animals, bleached white by the desert sun.

Still, in that dramatic scene when the prophet faces the valley of dry bones, God reveals the possibility of hope, even in the face of unnecessary death. As he is preaching, the prophet watches the bones rise and reconnect, joined by fresh tendons and muscles into new bodies. Before Ezekiel's eyes, God resurrects an army from the remains of those who had been rejected and consumed. White poverty's wounds do not only point us toward the connections between policies that are hurting all of us. If we face white poverty with Ezekiel's prophetic eye, it also reveals the potential power of poor people. Though they have been crushed and rejected, poor people are the new swing voters who can unite as the largest potential coalition to reconstruct democracy.

As I've listened to people like Lakin and Stanley and the women who started Taco Tuesdays, Ezekiel's vision in the valley of dry bones has been a sign to me that none of us should be too quick to compose an elegy for the white people who are being crushed by the violence of poverty in the richest nation in the history of the world. Yes, there are politicians who wave the bloody shirts of the dead to rally troops for reactionary extremism. There are so-called "cultural conservatives" who appeal to nostalgia for simpler times. There are policies that are crushing poor white people and leaving their communities desolate. But there is power in those communities. If they connect with other poor people, they can rise up as a nonviolent army to vote for an economy that works for all of us.

Yes, poor white people have been left for dead by a system that pretends to privilege them. But they do not need a hero to compose an elegy for them. From ancient times, elegies have been a way for public figures to stir public sentiment by remembering those who cannot speak for themselves. The ancient poets also had another artistic form for inviting others to share their enthusiasm for a vision of the good life. A rhapsody was an epic poem or song that aroused public sentiment not for an aching to return to the past, but for a shared longing to build a better future. From what I've seen, America needs a hillbilly *rhapsody* to celebrate the vision of poor white people who are refusing the old myths of division to join hands with the people they've been pitted against and reconstruct America. This is the song I hear poor white people singing all across this land, and it is the melody we must learn to sing with them. If we do not, they are vulnerable to populists who pretend to champion their interests while profiting off of their pain.

Take, for example, Senator J. D. Vance in Ohio. In 2016, his memoir, *Hillbilly Elegy*, became a best-selling book and conversation piece for Americans trying to understand white poverty and the appeal of the MAGA movement. Vance wrote about how his own life had been shaped by the poverty of rural Appalachia and his family's relocation to a Rust Belt town in Ohio. While he had been able, in many ways, to live the American Dream, serving in the military and attending Yale Law School, Vance shared about the forces of death that weighed on him and his family, telling stories about how the violence of his beloved Mamaw and Papaw's relationship echoed through the generations of their family.

"I'd like to tell you how my grandparents thrived in their new environment, how they raised a successful family, and how they retired comfortably middle-class," he confessed. "But that is a partial truth. The full truth is that my grandparents struggled in their new life, and they continued to do so for decades. Mamaw and Papaw may have made it out of Kentucky, but they and their children learned the hard way that Route 23 didn't lead where they hoped."

Vance's stories sound familiar. They echo the experiences of folks I've met in the mountains of North Carolina and the hills of Kentucky; in homeless encampments in rural Washington State and in the woods outside of Hickory, North Carolina, where a white woman without any teeth swept the dirt outside her tent to welcome me and a small delegation of visitors. She told us the story of how the furniture factories had left her town and the economy had dried up in the only place she'd ever known. She'd gone everywhere she knew to ask for help, and she'd worked every job she could find, but she was living in the woods with a group of friends who, like her, had no other place to call home. She told me she didn't know how long she was going to make it, but she asked if I would share her story, even if she did not survive to tell it herself. In America's valley of dry bones, she was clinging to hope that, one day, a movement could rise up to change the systems that had failed her.

There is something that feels noble about an elegy for people who have been crushed by white poverty in this country, but there's something dangerous about it, too. After all, when people are dead, they can no longer speak for themselves—and they certainly cannot make their voices heard at the ballot box.

Though Vance called himself a "never-Trump" conservative during the 2016 campaign and acknowledged that life was more difficult in Ohio steel towns after the factories left and the union jobs disappeared, he did not write his elegy to deal with the policy choices that have exacerbated poverty and led to unnecessary death for so many Americans. Instead, he leaned into the old myths and talked about the loss of character and diminishment of values in a so-called "culture of poverty." Vance said he wanted his book to be about "what goes on in the lives of real people when the industrial economy goes south. It's about reacting to bad circumstances in the worst way possible." Vance's ode to the grandparents who raised him, however moving and vulnerable, turned out to be a way of remembering the dead in order to rally support for his political career.

Having listened to hundreds of eulogies at the funerals where I have presided as a pastor, I can tell you this: the stories people tell about the dead are never just about the dead. They always make a case for what matters in the present and who we, as a people, want to be. In an election season, an elegy is often an appeal to voters.

In the fall of 2022, Vance was running for the U.S. Senate seat in Ohio. After struggling in the Republican primary in the spring, he had won the endorsement of Donald Trump and secured his place as the Republican candidate for a seat that Republican senator Rob Portman was leaving. After a summer with few public appearances, Vance was now holding rallies in small towns across Ohio, telling stories of growing up with his grandparents. In a campaign video, he walked down the street of his hometown with his shirtsleeves rolled up, criticizing his opponent for not being concerned about keeping Ohio's streets safe as a photo of his Mamaw appeared on the screen. With the familiar dog whistles of the Southern Strategy, Vance made his appeal to white voters.

I went to Cleveland, Ohio, with the Poor People's Campaign and marched through the city streets that Vance claimed were too dangerous for kids to play in. "Somebody's been stealing our healthcare," the crowd sang, "and it's gone on far too long." Poor people who were Black, white, and brown streamed into the Trinity Cathedral Episcopal Church a little east of downtown, lifting their voices together to fill its gothic arches with a yearning that echoed off the walls and pulsed through my body. They were determined to sing a new song about what is possible in America.

Teri, a white woman with blunt bangs and square jaw, introduced herself to the crowd as someone who wasn't well educated but had become self-educated by necessity. She had lived her whole life in the mountains of Kentucky that Vance's grandparents had left for work in Ohio. Teri knew hillbilly culture, but she explained how she refused to see her people and her place in the ways that the people who use them tried to make her. When her kids had to walk across coal muck in the road to get to their school bus stop, Teri called the coal company and told them they needed to come and clean up their mess. An employee on the other end of the line suggested she should just get used to it because this was a "coal community," but Teri was defiant.

"I don't live in a coal community," she told them. "It ain't like there's fields full of coal up here, and you can just walk through picking it up. I live in a mountain community that's been impacted by coal mining," Teri declared, setting the record straight. She wasn't going to let some corporation trying to make money redefine her and her place.

Over decades of standing up to the coal corporations, Teri had won awards from national and international environmental organizations. But she came to Cleveland that evening in 2022 to challenge the people who've praised her for her work to not just care about the environment, but to also join the Poor People's Campaign and commit to challenging all of the interlocking injustices that impact poor people in America. As Teri issued her challenge, folks who'd come in off the streets of Cleveland stood and cheered alongside pastors and workers, veterans and housing advocates. Looking around that cathedral full of poor people who'd gathered from the hood to the holler, Teri said, "My fantasy has always been, 'How can we get all these people together?' "

Teri knew she was looking at the kind of movement we need if we're going to win in the struggle to reconstruct an America that works for everyone. Yes, politicians like Vance have been able to win some white folks with nostalgic elegies and veiled appeals to racist fears. But they have also alienated a lot of poor white people—folks like Teri who understand that their political leaders aren't really serving them.

Whenever I meet someone like Teri, I know I'm connecting with family. Moral fusion is in my DNA, and when I hear someone singing its song, I can always sing along—even if it's an unfamiliar tune. I've met people who echo the harmonies of mountain populism in every Appalachian community I've ever visited. When we were in Corbin, the same day I met Lakin, as I described in Chapter 7, a bluegrass band came to the church and played "Will the Circle Be Unbroken?" I tapped my toe and sang along, thinking about the deep connections between the spiritual striving for eternal life "in the sky, Lord, in the sky" and the longing of dry bones for a movement that can raise them up into a nonviolent army that's able to transform the death-dealing systems of this world here and now.

Even in the local music, fusion is a part of mountain culture. Folk songs from Scotland and Ireland have been passed down through generations of bluegrass pickers in the hollers of Kentucky, Virginia, West Virginia, Tennessee, and North Carolina. But right there in the middle of every jam session in the hills of Appalachia is the banjo—an instrument brought to the South by enslaved Africans. It's easy to get overwhelmed by the power of the old myths, but when we listen closely to the songs of America, fusion is all around us.

Every chance I get to hear somebody sing a hillbilly rhapsody restores my soul. Teri is my sister, and my faith tells me that the America we dream together must be. Still, I know that data are not the plural of an anecdote. We witnessed a glimpse of Teri's moral fusion fantasy in that church in Cleveland, but Vance still won the Senate seat. It takes more than personal connections to transform a society, though every relationship that binds us is essential. Change requires movement-building. We cannot become the nation we have never yet been without the power to enact better policies. Poor people of every race, region, and religion must rise up from their valleys of dry bones, rally and march, protest and vote for better opportunities for themselves and their families. Every moral fusion movement that has pushed America toward higher ground has won its demands by building power.

We don't just need a better song to sing—a new story that tells us who we really are and who we might yet become as a nation. We also need a plan to win. Through Ezekiel's eyes, I see a path to victory through mobilizing a nonviolent army of poor voters.

Nationwide, the 2018 midterms saw a roughly 10 percent increase in voter participation over the previous midterms—a larger four-year increase than Obama's record-breaking turnout in 2008. Many factors contributed to this surge in participation, but from our work on the ground in almost every state, the Poor People's Campaign knew that a raw number increase in low-income voters made a significant contribution to the "blue wave" that returned control of the U.S. House to Democrats in 2018 and put a check on Trump's use of the White House to reward elite interests and undermine policies that lift poor people. Our campaign had not done partisan organizing, but we had talked to enough poor people to know that, if they showed up, they wouldn't vote for things to stay the way they were. And they hadn't. As we organized to build a movement, we didn't just invite people to tell their stories and march. We invited them to join a movement that votes, and we gave poor people ways to talk to their family and neighbors about the issues at stake in the election. We knew it was a winning strategy that would be successful if we could scale up this form of organizing.

This strategy was counterintuitive to the pundits and political observers who had attributed the rise of the MAGA movement to an insurgent "populism." Reporters who chased the campaign rallies that never really took a pause during Trump's four years in the White House posted a steady stream of videos that demonstrated the extremism of MAGA enthusiasts. By every account, those crowds were overwhelmingly white. They never represented, however, the majority of poor people who voted. In the 2016 election, Donald Trump won every income bracket above $50,000 by 1 to 4 points, but he lost every bracket below $50,000 by more than 9 points. I knew that the "non-college-educated white voter" that pollsters kept talking about wasn't someone like Teri who'd watched coal companies and politicians sell out her community. He or she was, more often than not, the small business owner or the retired person who believed the story that said everyone will eventually be better off if their taxes stay low and their 401(k) keeps growing.

The data made it clear that poor people were not driving the extremism in American politics, nor were they the true base for a president whose major policy achievement was to cut taxes for corporations and wealthy Americans. In fact, we began to argue that poor people were the key to stopping the madness. The elusive "independent swing voter" wasn't going to rescue American democracy. We needed a movement to engage people who hadn't voted because they've never imagined the system could work for them. Poor people were the voters who could swing any election.

I learned a long time ago that if you're going to be loud, you'd better not be wrong. So our campaign did its homework. We asked some of the scholars who know the data on low-propensity voters to run the numbers and tell us what was possible. In a report titled "Unleashing the Power of Poor and Low-Income Americans," Columbia University's Rob Hartley outlined how low-income voter turnout over the previous 36 years had been consistently 20 percentage points below that of higher-income voters. According to his estimates, these obstacles had combined with an array of voter suppression measures to keep 34 million poor Americans from voting in 2016.

If poor people voted at levels similar to their higher-income neighbors, their voting power could not only flip the swing states Trump won across the Rust Belt. According to Hartley's analysis, they could also crack the "Solid South" that Republicans have counted on for decades by flipping North Carolina, Georgia, Florida, Mississippi, Texas, and Arizona. The key is building a movement that can persuade political candidates to speak directly to this potential electorate, championing an agenda that would improve the lot of most Americans. Poor people aren't the problem in America's democracy. They are the sleeping giant that, if awakened, could decide the future of the nation.

But why do many poor people not vote? When surveyed, eligible non-voters across income brackets choose the same top two reasons for not voting: they don't feel they are represented by the candidates who are running or they do not think their vote would make a difference. For poor people, it's no surprise that they wouldn't feel represented by candidates who refuse to say the word "poor." Republicans try to appeal to them by claiming to represent their values, and Democrats sometimes call them people "aspiring to the middle class." But you can't feed hungry children values and aspirations. If you're working two jobs to make ends meet and you never know what your schedule is going to be the second Tuesday in November, showing up to cast a ballot for someone who doesn't speak to your situation isn't a priority.

A movement can change how candidates talk and what agenda they promise to pursue when elected. If a moral fusion movement, led by poor people, could rise up in America today, the data say we have the numbers to change the political calculus. As a campaign, we knew we couldn't do everything, but we wanted to test this strategy for organizing. We turned our attention to mobilizing this new electorate in a signal election in 2019.

Governor Matt Bevin of Kentucky was an unpopular incumbent at the time who had embraced austerity measures that hurt a broad cross section of low-income Kentuckians. Still, he had the endorsement of President Trump, who had won Kentucky by 30 points just three years earlier. The Kentucky Poor People's Campaign joined a coalition of groups to go into poor communities across the state and train people of every race to talk to other poor people like them about what was at stake in the election. Poor Black residents of Lexington and Louisville linked up with poor white coal miners from Appalachia, and they went door-to-door in their own communities. They held events at their community centers and in their homes; they used their cell phones to text and call folks who political campaigns never reach out to because they haven't voted in recent elections or may not even be registered. They didn't talk about candidates or political parties. They talked about building power for poor people through a movement that pushed policies for the good of the whole and votes for candidates who champion those policies. Ending the violence of policy murder, they said, wasn't a left or right issue. It was a moral issue in the state of Kentucky.

Governor Bevin continued to use the tropes of Christian nationalism to cast his pro-corporate policies as "pro-life," but everyday Kentuckians kept speaking out to say that healthcare, living wages, and voting rights were the moral issues that mattered to them. Trump traveled to Lexington and stumped for Bevin. "If you lose," he said to the governor, "it sends a really bad message. You can't let that happen to me."

On election night, Bevin looked worried as results came in and it became clear that the race was tighter than most people had thought it would be. His Democratic challenger, Andy Beshear, had embraced the policies our campaign was raising with poor people, and he had adopted some of the moral language we were using. As counties reported their vote tallies, it was clear that Kentucky's large cities, which Democrats always win, had turned out strong numbers for Beshear. As the night grew long, the question became whether those bases of support could outweigh Bevin's base in the rural counties. With an overall turnout nearly 14 percentage points higher than four years earlier, Beshear garnered 5,100 more total votes than Bevin, pulling off an upset. He gave his victory speech to an enthusiastic crowd that included Kentuckians from every walk of life. His young kids, standing beside him, were up way past their bedtime to witness a historic moment: a movement of new voters had awakened to elect their dad and push for policies that would lift everyone in their state.

As Beshear thanked his supporters, he declared that the people of Kentucky had proven that "elections don't have to be about Right versus Left; they are still about right versus wrong." The song the poor people had been singing all across the state was now echoing in the victory speech of their new governor.

While Kentucky's surge of voter participation was as high as 17 percent in the typical Democratic strongholds of Fayette and Jefferson counties, an increase of 15 to 17 percentage points in rural Kenton, Scott, Campbell, and Warren counties flipped areas of the state that had long been considered reliably "red." Even in rural counties that Bevin won, new voters had narrowed the margin of victory, contributing to the total vote count that made Beshear's victory possible. These rural counties that were supposed to be Bevin's base were the hollers where poor white people had been talking to one another about new possibilities and singing the new song of moral fusion on front porches. This is where the McCoys had been telling their people, "They've been playing us against one another." It's where sister Teri had, in fighting the coal companies, begun to ask, "What might happen if we could get all these people together?" In the valleys of Kentucky's hills, dry bones were rattling.

Beshear defeated Bevin not only because of an increased turnout in urban "blue" counties, but also because a higher turnout of poor white voters changed the landscape in so-called "red" counties. In a race that was decided by 5,100 votes, he could not have won without the increased turnout in rural, majority white counties. Not every victory can be won in a single election cycle, but Kentucky in 2019 was a signal that the hillbilly rhapsody we'd been hearing across Appalachia was more than a song of inspiration; it could also become the anthem of a movement to change the nation. We needed to invest in scaling up this model of moral fusion organizing to build a poor people's movement that votes.

The 2020 federal election gave the Poor People's Campaign an opportunity to take what we'd seen in Kentucky and apply it across the country. If poor people could defy the old myth's lies and come together to awaken a new electorate, they had the power to pick presidents. But if the thousands of people committed to organizing with our campaign were going to awaken millions of their neighbors, we had to compel presidential candidates to speak directly to poor people and low-wage workers. We had to get them to address the issues threatening poor people's lives.

During the primary season, I sent an invitation to everyone who was running for president to come to a poverty forum at the church I pastored, a brick building with an A-frame roof that sits across a two-lane highway from a Dollar General store in a community where most of the children qualify for free or reduced-cost lunch. These wouldn't be campaign events. They would be community forums following our congregation's regular worship services. We didn't want to hear the candidates' stump speeches. We wanted them to listen to poor people share about the issues weighing directly on them and their communities. And we wanted the candidates to explain how they planned to address living wages and access to healthcare, voter suppression, and ecological devastation in communities like ours.

Several candidates agreed, and we were overwhelmed by the turnout, opening the community center behind the Dollar General for the overflow crowd of folks who wanted to hear how candidates would address the issues that mattered to them. We broadcast these conversations to people across the nation who'd joined the Poor People's Campaign, and we invited everyday people who'd signed on to be part of a movement that votes to host watch parties in their homes and communities. When Senator Bernie Sanders came, people stayed for an hour and a half of dialogue after our Ash Wednesday service, clearly energized by the back-and-forth between a politician and poor people.

Senator Sanders told me at the end of the evening that he'd had more conversations about things that matter to everyday Americans in those ninety minutes than he'd had in all the televised primary debates combined.

"Well, if that's the case," I said, "then we're in trouble, because this is what we ought to be talking about."

It dawned on me that candidates for the highest office in the land face the same narrative problem that moral fusion movements have confronted throughout our nation's history. The structures of our political process focus them on hot-button issues that differentiate candidates from their opponents rather than calling them to address the pressing issues of our time. When given a chance to talk about poverty, low wages, healthcare, and voting rights as issues that intersect to impoverish our democracy, they had something to say. And poor people were eager to hear it.

When Pete Buttigieg, then the mayor of South Bend, Indiana, came to a similar forum after a Sunday morning worship service in December 2019, he addressed the silence about poverty in our politics directly. "Rev, I'm probably not supposed to say this. I might get in trouble for sharing it here. But the reason we don't talk about poverty is that the consultants tell us not to."

I appreciated his honesty. It clarified for me that the dry bones of this nation who want to rise together and sing a new song are not only fighting the distractions and divisions of culture wars. In the struggle to shift the moral narrative in American politics, we're also up against a multi-million-dollar industry that advises Democrats to avoid speaking directly to poor people. Yet, despite this advice, candidates responded to a movement of poor people and low-wage workers who challenged them to speak directly to them. Our folks weren't turned off by the word "poor." They were fired up to hear the people they saw on television each night finally talking to them.

When the COVID-19 pandemic shut down in-person gatherings in March 2020, we knew that we had to find ways to keep pushing candidates to address poverty. For all of their lives, poor folks in our campaign had been called "low-wage workers." Now that a deadly virus threatened them and their families every day as they went to work on public transit, delivered groceries, cared for people in nursing homes, and processed mail orders in distribution centers, they had a new title: "essential workers." Neighbors who were sheltering in place at home came out on their porches each evening and rang bells to celebrate workers who were keeping them alive for less than a living wage. Still, our government didn't mandate that the people we called "essential" receive the things essential to their survival. "They call us essential," a woman who worked as an assistant in a nursing home said to me, "but I feel expendable." She not only lacked the personal protective equipment she needed to do her job safely. She wept as she said she couldn't afford to pay her bills if she did get sick and missed fourteen days of work for quarantine.

Months later, when the data came in, we would learn that lower-income Americans died at as much as five times the rate of their wealthier neighbors during the worst waves of the pandemic. One study found that as many as 330,000 Americans died not simply from the disease, but because they lacked access to the healthcare they needed to survive it. Poor people didn't need to wait for the data to know this. One member of our campaign in Mississippi told me she lost 20 members of her family within a 30-mile radius. As a pastor, I knew that she had to find space to grieve.

"Don't worry if you need to take a break from organizing," I told her over the phone. "Other people can step in."

But she said she couldn't stop. "This movement is the only family I've got left." Mobilizing poor people for a movement that could reconstruct democracy was the work that was keeping her alive.

The poor people and low-wage workers organizing with us to mobilize a new electorate were not the only folks wrestling with the ways Americans seemed particularly vulnerable to a pandemic. As the 2020 election approached, public health officials struggled to explain why the COVID death rate in the United States was so much higher than in other nations with comparable resources and access to vaccines. Democrats blamed Trump and other Republicans who failed to follow the advice of public health officials. Researchers also pointed to the role of systemic racism in healthcare disparities. But race and partisan politics alone could not explain the disparity. America was uniquely vulnerable among the wealthy nations of the world because America leads its peers in the percentage of our population that we allow to live in poverty. Poor voters, more than anyone, could see what was at stake in this election.

Then, in the summer of 2020, Americans who'd been isolating to try to avoid a deadly respiratory disease watched a seventeen-year-old's video footage of Minneapolis police officer Derek Chauvin choking the life out of George Floyd while Floyd cried, "I can't breathe." It touched a shared nerve and inspired a collective gasp for democracy. People took to the streets, embracing the "Black Lives Matter" slogan and marching for justice in what would become the largest mass demonstration in U.S. history. A nonviolent army rose up to raise a general lament.

As we continued to mobilize a moral fusion movement of poor voters, I noted that, while Floyd was Black and the officer choking him was white, the crowds that marched in cities and towns across the nation were as diverse as any fusion coalition in our shared history. Their chants of "I can't breathe" were not just a protest against racist policing; they were a cry for life from people who were seeing unnecessary deaths all around them. Yes, Floyd was a Black man. He was also a low-wage worker who'd relocated to Minneapolis in search of better work. The movement that rose up in his name was a collective chant that harmonized with the rhapsody I'd heard in Appalachia. All of the people singing this shared song were potential members of the coalition we needed to reconstruct democracy.

That June, I went to the National Cathedral in Washington, D.C., and preached a sermon titled "America, Accepting

Death Is No Longer an Option." I took as my text the passage from the prophet Amos that says, "Go out into the streets and lament loudly! Fill the malls and shops with cries of doom! Weep loudly, 'Not me! Not us, not now!' Empty offices, stores, factories, workplaces. Enlist everyone in the general lament."

The ancient prophet had called for a direct action that was in fact happening in our streets—a general lament for the many thousands gone. We weren't just mourning the murder of George Floyd or the untold unnecessary deaths from COVID. Our general lament was a cry against our nation's addiction to unnecessary death, I preached. The heirs of generations of genocide, displacement, enslavement, and lynching, we, as a people, had never repented of the violence that was laid as a foundation for our shared life. Instead, we'd accustomed ourselves to an economy that functions by damning some people to die before their time.

For far too long, many of us had believed the old myth that says unnecessary death only happens to "those people"—others who we blame for their poverty or race, their "high-crime community" or immigration status. But COVID was acting like a contrast dye to expose how deep poverty runs throughout our society, impacting so many of us, without regard for race or creed. And where this disease overwhelmed our health-care system's capacity to respond to sick people, all of us were suddenly vulnerable.

Our addiction to unnecessary death, we could now see, threatened *every* American life.

The prophet Amos promised that, if we would engage in a general lament, God would hear from heaven and act to bring justice. Our responsibility, I said, was to tell the truth and confess our wrongdoing—past and present—that created public policies with such high death measurements. Amid a national uprising in the streets, I preached that a moral fusion movement had to insist that accepting unnecessary death is no longer an option. We had to come together and vote together for an economy in which everyone can thrive.

The following Saturday, on June 18, 2020, the Poor People's Campaign held our National Assembly and Moral March on Washington. We had been planning it for over a year, but when emergency declarations forbade large public gatherings earlier that spring, I had called our planning committee and said we would have to postpone.

"We can't," they said. "COVID is killing people, but poverty has been killing us for a lot longer. We have to find a way to do this."

I didn't know how we'd do it, but we had decided in that meeting that we would find a way. It reminded me of the question God asks Ezekiel when he first shows him the valley of dry bones. "Can these bones live?"

"Only you know," Ezekiel replies. I wasn't sure how we could build a platform for the dry bones of America to come together in the midst of a public health emergency, but I knew we could only find a way by pressing forward. If we were going to mobilize a coalition that could win for poor and working people, we had to find a way to make the voices of poor people heard.

We took seriously the prophet's call to "enlist everyone" in our lament. Black, Indigenous, Asian, and Latino sisters and brothers needed to tell the truth about how racism and poverty have impacted their communities and killed their loved ones. So did poor white folks from Appalachia and the Midwest, from upstate New York and the Tenderloin, who have felt the pain of policy violence and unnecessary death. Working with a production company, we developed a plan that would allow dozens of people to share their stories via video feed from their communities. While many Americans were still sheltering in place, we partnered with C-SPAN and hundreds of national and grassroots partners' social media accounts to bring our virtual assembly into their homes. By the end of the weekend, more than 1.2 million people had participated on Facebook alone. We'd engaged far more people than we would have ever been able to get to D.C. Poor folks who live with their back against the wall knew that raising a movement from a valley of dry bones was impossible. "But we have to," they'd said. And they did it.

A few months later, after Republicans and Democrats had gathered for national conventions to nominate their candidates for president, we invited both Donald Trump and Joe Biden to address a virtual poverty forum as the pandemic continued to inhibit in-person gatherings in most communities across the United States. The Trump campaign opted not to participate, but then-candidate Biden addressed our assembly. If he were elected, he pledged, "ending poverty will not just be an aspiration; it will be a theory of change to build a new economy that includes everyone."

Weeks later in November, more than 80 million voters delivered the most definitive rebuke of a sitting president since FDR defeated Herbert Hoover in 1932. Joe Biden had promised to champion a $15 minimum wage and affordable healthcare for all—issues that mattered to poor people everywhere. In the midst of an economic crisis, a pandemic, and an uprising for racial justice, poor people and low-wage workers of every hue responded in record numbers to overwhelm the reactionary base that Donald Trump had stoked with lies and fear.

When our research team told me that at least six million more low-income people had voted in 2020 than in 2016, I knew we were witnessing something larger than the results of our efforts alone. Our campaign had worked hard to educate people and send them out to mobilize their neighbors, but this surge in poor voters was bigger than anything we could have orchestrated. Six million new voters who earn less than $50,000 chose Biden over Trump by as many as 15 percentage points. In Florida, voters had the chance to cast their ballot not just for candidates, but also to raise the minimum wage to $15 an hour. In a state that Trump won, the measure passed with more votes than Trump or Biden received.

Poor white voters had joined Black, brown, and Native voters as well as anti-Trump voters in the suburbs to meet and surpass the turnout of Trump's base. In the midst of a pandemic, more people showed up to vote than ever before in U.S. history. A new electorate made up of poor people of every race was emerging to enact the fantasy Teri had shared in Ohio and insist that another America is possible. From among the dry bones of people who experience the violence of low wages and homelessness, a lack of access to healthcare and underfunded schools, a new movement was rising to sing a better song.

We had witnessed the power of a moral fusion movement that could unite people across the old dividing lines, but our work wasn't finished. If history had taught us anything, we knew we had to prepare ourselves for the inevitable backlash that the forces aligned against us were already planning.

Chapter 9

WHY WE MUST LIFT
FROM THE BOTTOM

A s President-elect Biden put together his transition team and began to talk about plans to "build back better" after winning the 2020 election, our campaign made the case that their language of reconstruction had to be backed up by a commitment to lift from the bottom. Where I'm from in northeastern North Carolina, I learned this lesson about rebuilding a long time ago. Storms coming in off the Atlantic Ocean can cause the water in our rivers and canals to rise, and folks who had built their homes too close to the water's edge sometimes realized they had to rebuild to keep from losing the house. In short, they had to build back better.

Whenever they moved a house back home, they always started by getting up under the foundation and jacking the whole structure up so they could put supports underneath and lift from the bottom. If you try to lift a house from the top, you'll pull the roof off. If you try to wrap something around it and lift from the middle, the whole thing will crack and come apart. But if you lift from the bottom, the whole structure can be moved to higher ground.

This is the basic message we tried to drive home to the incoming administration: if they really wanted to build back better, they needed to start by fulfilling their promises to raise the minimum wage, defend union rights, expand access to healthcare, and protect voting rights for all Americans. "When you lift from the bottom," we said, "everyone rises."

While we were making this case in our public meetings, in op-eds, and in media interviews, I got a message from a member of Biden's transition team. He was calling to ask if I would deliver the inaugural sermon at the service that the National Cathedral hosts for the president and vice president on their first morning in office. This wasn't the response I'd expected.

"If I were to do it, I'd have to be myself," I told him.

That's what they were asking, he said. "If you are willing, we want to ask if you'd consider preaching the text from Isaiah that calls us to be 'repairers of the breach.'"

"Well, I've got a few things to say about that," I said with a chuckle. And I accepted the invitation.

I knew that Isaiah's memorable phrase had a history in politics. President Bill Clinton's speechwriters often turned to the biblical call for "repairers of the breach" when they wanted to evoke a spirit of unity among Americans of very different backgrounds. Images of the U.S. Capitol under siege during the January 6 insurrection were still playing on the news every night as I prayed about how to preach the prophet's call. Biden had run on the promise that he could unify the country, but Trump's most ardent supporters seemed willing to burn the government down before they would hand it over to a new administration.

A call to unity was needed, but not just any kind of unity. A mob can unite around evil, as it does at a Klan rally. A crowd can be unified for a good time, as it is at a concert or festival. But if we were going to get to the kind of unity Isaiah envisioned, we had to go back earlier in his prophecy and pay attention to the conditions of the Lord's promise. "*If* you loose the bands of wickedness," Isaiah says—a phrase that some of my rabbi friends say is best translated from the Hebrew as "*If* you pay people a living wage." If you care for the poor and make them the center of your attention—if you even invite them into your home and treat them like family, the prophet says—"*then* your light will break forth like the dawn and your healing will be complete." Only *then*, Isaiah says, will you be called a "repairer of the breach."

Public health protocols in January 2021 still prevented indoor gatherings in Washington, D.C., so President Biden, Vice President Kamala Harris, and their families and senior staff would be masked and socially distanced in the State Dining Room of the White House for the service. I was to address them and the nation by video feed from a pulpit in Raleigh, North Carolina. It was a strange experience, walking into an empty sanctuary to preach the prophet's message to the nation. I sat down on a stool behind the pulpit before the camera went live and centered myself while a gospel pianist played the old hymn "Must Jesus Bear the Cross Alone?" I knew I wasn't alone. The same God who'd inspired the prophet to write the vision in ancient Israel was with me in twenty-first-century America. What's more, I knew a movement was rising among poor people to make this message heard. I wasn't here because I'd mastered the lessons I'd learned all those years ago in preaching class. I was here to sing the song that was rising up from America's valley of dry bones. I remembered something my daddy had told me years before: for a preacher, the question isn't whether you have access to power, but what you chose to do with the access you have.

I stepped into the pulpit, asked God to help me, and looked into the camera lens that stood on a tripod in the middle of that sanctuary. "The breach, according to the imagery of Isaiah," I said, "is when there is a gap in the nation between what is and how God wants things to be. Transposed to our time, the breach is when we say, 'one nation under God, indivisible' with our lips while we see the rich and the poor living in two very different Americas."

I told the president that I knew he'd felt the breach personally, facing poverty as a child when his father lost his job. I told the vice president that I knew she, too, had felt the sting of racism's breach in America's common life. "Even what we saw happen at the Capitol two weeks ago is the results of a long history . . . This strategy of feeding and seeding intentional division into the body politic spilled over into the inevitable violence that ideas of supremacy always produce." Isaiah's vision exposed the old myths and illuminated the fact that our obvious lack of unity was rooted in the old breaches of racism and poverty.

The job of a preacher is, in some ways, like the work of a surgeon. You have to get down to the cause of the illness before you can apply the medicine. I knew that if we, as a nation, could face the real source of our breaches, the prophet had good news for all of us. "If we the people, with God's help, repair the breach, revival and renewal will come," I preached. "Love and light will burst through. God will hear our prayers if we do the work of repairing society's breach. No, America has never yet been all that she has hoped to be. But right here, right now, a Third Reconstruction is possible."

This wasn't just wishful thinking. I was preaching a vision for society that Isaiah had seen thousands of years ago. I was also preaching what I had seen in Mitchell County and Belhaven, North Carolina; in Corbin and Harlan counties in Kentucky. Powerful forces were at work to persuade us that the country was hopelessly divided, but the good news I preached on the president's first day in office was that we might, in fact, be on the cusp of a new birth of freedom.

Rather than just respond to the extremism of people who were spreading lies about a stolen election, our staff at Repairers of the Breach worked to keep the focus on the agenda that a majority of American voters had united to endorse in the 2020 election. If Republicans were willing to go along with lies about "election integrity" to try to undermine democracy, Democrats had a responsibility to use the power they'd been entrusted with to defend democracy and pass policies that addressed poverty and low wages. When we met at the White House with President Biden's economic advisors, our group included two dozen poor people from every race and region to explain why policies that lift from the bottom are not "far left" or "radical" proposals; they are the solutions most Americans want for the problems that plague our communities.

Sarah, a white mother of seven and grandmother of six from Durham, North Carolina, told Biden's advisors about working at Waffle House for what she called "poverty wages." As White House officials were still preparing their pandemic response, Sarah told them, "I don't have paid sick days. I don't have hazard pay, and I don't have healthcare. I've never been able to find a job that pays a living wage." Here was a white worker who'd linked up with Black and brown service workers in the South, pleading with her government to repair the breaches that threatened to consume her family. She said she had just voted for the first time in her life because she believed what President Biden had said about raising the federal minimum wage to $15 an hour. Now, she wanted to see the administration make that promise a reality for millions of workers like her.

Yes, some white people caught up in the old myths were willing to storm the Capitol and try to overthrow the will of the new multiethnic majority in America. But those people weren't Sarah and her increasingly large ilk. They weren't most people, even in the South, where James Crow, Esquire had worked overtime for years, as we've seen, to try to divide moral fusion coalitions and prevent America's new majority from exercising its collective will. What is so tellingly forgotten in the media is that the evening before a few thousand people stormed the U.S. Capitol on January 6, more than 2.2 million people turned out in a special election in Georgia to elect Rev. Dr. Raphael Warnock and Jon Ossoff to the U.S. Senate. Black and white together, images of Warnock and Ossoff represented the fusion coalition that had not only elected them, but also had given Democrats in the Senate a majority to make Biden's promises real for people like Sarah by passing legislation to raise the federal minimum wage.

Before the White House and Senate leadership could finish their plan to pass a minimum wage increase, however, Senator Joe Manchin from West Virginia started talking to reporters about why he did not support it. A few years earlier, when

Democrats were in the minority in the Senate, I had addressed their caucus. Rather than speak by myself, I insisted on taking two low-wage workers with me—one Black and one white. Senator Manchin had called me after our session and expressed how moved he had been to hear me talk about the plight of poor white folks in West Virginia. We'd talked about the shared struggles of poor people and the need to work together for policy solutions. I'd hoped back then that he could be an ally to our movement.

Now that Democrats had a majority in the Senate, Manchin was suggesting that a higher minimum wage could hurt working people from his state, even though a $15 minimum wage was part of the national platform of his own party. Though economists have debunked these claims, I knew they were the talking points he was getting from the U.S. Chamber of Commerce. We needed more than data to combat their false narrative. We needed someone who could push back against these lies from personal experience and in language that everyday people in West Virginia understand. I knew I needed to call my friend Pam Garrison.

I first met Pam in the Zoom rooms that became so familiar during the pandemic, on an organizing call with members of the Poor People's Campaign from West Virginia. She had teamed up with a Black woman from Charleston and organized poor women across their state. Pam is a straight-talking white mountain woman who has struggled to survive poverty her whole life. I remembered her saying that first time we'd talked that she'd learned a long time ago to roll change—putting spare nickels and dimes in paper sleeves—to get up enough gas money to make it to her next minimum-wage job in the mountains, where public transportation isn't an option. If Manchin was going to parrot the neoliberal lies about the minimum wage, he needed to answer directly to constituents like Pam.

We organized a West Virginia delegation in early 2021 to meet with Manchin. He seemed visibly surprised when he saw that most of the faces of the West Virginians who'd come with me to meet him were white. Mostly older women, they didn't waste any time getting to the point. "Senator Manchin, I knew your momma," one of them said. "I know where you come from, and I can't believe you're treating poor people like this."

Pam made clear what was at stake. "The minimum wage has never been sufficient to feed my family and to survive on," she told Manchin. "This is supposed to be a rescue package. Well, you can't take the biggest part of the rescue out."

Manchin did what politicians so often do. He thanked the women who'd shared their personal stories of pain and talked about the poverty he had seen as a young person in West Virginia. Then he told them that he thought he had worked out a compromise with some Republican colleagues that could get the minimum wage up to maybe $12 an hour. But those women were absolutely clear: Democrats had made a promise, and they expected Manchin to keep it.

If poor people had decided that coming together to defeat an extremist Republican was in their best interest, they were equally clear that we had to challenge so-called moderate Democrats who refused to recognize the severity of poverty and income inequality. I was reminded of Dr. Martin Luther King Jr.'s reflection in his letter from the Birmingham City Jail. "I have almost reached the regrettable conclusion that the Negro's great stumbling block in the stride toward freedom is not the

White Citizens Councilor or the Ku Klux Klanner," he wrote, "but the white moderate who is more devoted to 'order' than to justice."

Pam shared the analysis Dr. King had made more than a half century earlier. Attention to the pain and suffering that is part of the normal order of things allowed them both to see that justice is not some middle ground between people who are fighting for their lives and politicians who defend the status quo. When a fire is threatening human lives, a moderate response from someone who has the power to extinguish the flames is violence. A politician like Joe Manchin could say he wanted to be "bipartisan," insisting that the way to unity was through compromise with his Republican colleagues. But face-to-face with constituents like Pam, Manchin looked like someone who cared more about the well-being of his wealthy donors than of his poor constituents from West Virginia.

Still, the narrative on Capitol Hill kept coming back to whether someone like Manchin could negotiate a reasonable compromise between the deeply divided Democrats and Republicans. I could see that the agenda we had worked so hard to get Democrats to endorse was going to be blocked by Manchin and his colleague from Arizona, Kyrsten Sinema, who was also backing away from the president's commitments in the name of bipartisanship. We had worked hard in our fusion organizing to make the connection between policies that lift poor people, like living wages, and policies that expand and protect democracy, like restoring the Voting Rights Act. If policies that created greater inequality over decades were the result of an impoverished democracy, we argued, then we could not hope for legislation that would reconstruct democracy unless we restored and expanded voting rights protections. While higher wages were often framed as a "class issue" that poor white people should care about, voting rights were almost always framed as a "Black issue"—something that civil rights organizations had fought for that impacted mostly Black people. The multiracial movement we'd built was confronting this false dichotomy, rooted in the old myths. It had united poor white people with their poor Black neighbors to vote for leaders who said they would fight for living wage *and* voting rights. We needed both at the same time if we were going to truly lift from the bottom.

Manchin's extreme position made this connection clearer to the people of West Virginia than any political education materials Repairers of the Breach had been able to produce up until that point. After Manchin said he would block raising the minimum wage, he then announced that he was also refusing to join the Democratic majority to override the Republican filibuster and pass the For the People Act—the voting rights legislation that Representative John Lewis had championed in the last years of his life.

No single representative in American public life embodied the fight for voting rights more than John Lewis. After he challenged Democrats to back living wages and voting rights at the March on Washington in 1963, a twenty-three-year-old Lewis went to Selma, Alabama, to support a grassroots campaign for voting rights there. He led Black and white voting rights advocates on a march across the Edmund Pettus Bridge and was brutally beaten by officers on horseback who charged the nonviolent marchers. After he was elected to the U.S. House of Representatives in 1986, Lewis championed the voting rights he'd spilled his own blood to win for more than three decades in Congress.

Then, after the *Shelby* decision in 2013 unleashed a host of voter suppression bills in statehouses across the country, Lewis worked hard with his colleagues in the House and Senate to put together an omnibus bill that would protect and extend voting rights for all Americans, over and against the multipronged attacks of James Crow, Esquire. Before Lewis's death in 2020, Manchin had signed on as a cosponsor of his For the People Act in the U.S. Senate. Now, less than a year later, Manchin said he didn't believe the Senate should proceed with voting rights legislation on a party-line vote. As with living wages, this meant that Democrats in the Senate would do nothing to enact the agenda they had run on. Meanwhile, according to the Brennan Center, more than 250 proposed changes to voting laws had been introduced by Republicans in state legislatures across the United States in the winter and spring of 2021. The fire of voter suppression was raging, and Senator Manchin said he didn't believe he should do anything to put it out until he could persuade the arsonists to join him.

Pam called me again from West Virginia and said we had to march. "They always say voter suppression is about hurting Black people, Reverend Barber, but they're pushing these laws up here in West Virginia, and we ain't hardly got no Black people."

Pam was right. The nation needed to see poor white folks challenging their own senator on wages and voting rights. This was much bigger than West Virginia. Our organizers at Repairers of the Breach told me folks in Arizona wanted to plan a sit-in in Senator Sinema's office to demand that she keep her promises and support the White House plan to lift from the bottom by raising the minimum wage and protecting voting rights. Down in Texas, where the state legislature was taking up legislation to roll back voting rights, we heard from a coalition that wanted to march to the capital in the summer heat to draw attention to the extremism that was happening in statehouses while a couple of senators refused to act. I got another call from my friend, the country music artist Willie Nelson. Years ago, I got to know Willie through the work he does to support farmers in rural America through an organization called Farm Aid. Willie understands how voter suppression impacts not only the people it targets, but also the farmers who can't get politicians to pass the policies we need to support a sustainable food system. Willie said he would invite all his friends to join us at the statehouse in Austin at the end of the march, and we ended up having a Texas-size rally—more than 10,000 people standing together to demand a government that works for the people and lifts from the bottom.

This was the pathway to the unity that so many yearned for—the healing that an unprecedented number of voters had hoped for when they gave Democrats control of the House, the Senate, and the White House. The 2020 multiethnic uprising for racial justice, in which Black, white, and brown had marched together, had helped galvanize a fusion coalition committed to greater equity in America. A year later, "anti-woke" campaigns waged by organizations flush with mystery money were stoking the old myths, claiming that anti-racism efforts were an attack on white people. So-called "parents' rights" organizations were arguing that Black history could hurt white kids, and extremist legislators were trying to ban books that tell the truth about our shared history of inequality. We didn't need to figure out how to compromise with that. We needed a fusion movement of Black and white people standing together to demand that the nation address the real breach between those who enjoy the bounty of America's prosperity and the 140 million poor people of every race who, like Sarah and Pam, aren't sure how they're going to make it day-to-day.

We needed to help people see that America's long fight for equality is not a zero-sum game. West Virginia, I began to see, was our Selma.

If Black and white people marching for voting rights in Alabama's Black Belt in 1965 had exposed the inherent violence of Jim Crow for all Americans to see, then poor white people marching for voting rights and living wages with their Black and brown allies in West Virginia had the potential to unveil the violence of Manchin's extremism and the reactionary right's "war on woke." We hadn't worked this hard for this long to build a multiracial fusion movement just to watch the whole nation be distracted by some half-rate impersonations of Joseph McCarthy and George Wallace. And we sure weren't going to sit by quietly while the people who promised to represent us said we needed to be patient while they worked out a compromise with that nonsense. Right-wing extremists and so-called "moderate" Democrats were working in concert to thwart the will of the majority of Americans and prevent poor white people from earning higher wages alongside their poor Black and brown neighbors. We had to help the nation see what was really at stake.

I rode up to Charleston, West Virginia, in June 2021 and

joined a crowd that Pam and her friends had rallied to confront Manchin on his own turf, where he'd have to answer to his own constituents for his turn against the agenda that he'd promised to champion. We met under a highway overpass, down by the river, and West Virginians shared their own stories of not being able to make ends meet. As a tri-chair of the state Poor People's Campaign steering committee, Pam made clear why we'd come together. "The American people have been played for gullible fools—we have. And it's time we woke up! And it's time we woke our fellow Americans up before all we've got is a shell of a democracy." Pam told the crowd that we were going to march to Manchin's office.

In a line that stretched as far as the eye could see, we set out two-by-two. Ninety percent of the folks who were marching that day were white, but a few Black folks who'd come pulled me aside and said, "We wanted to show up for voting rights when we heard the call, but we've never been part of a group like this before." I smiled and told them, "Well, it's time."

As we made our way to the office, I learned that it was located in the state lottery building, across the street from a hospital. "It's almost like he admits that he's playing a game of chance with our lives," one woman said as we approached the building. When we arrived, the doors of the building were locked, and we were turned away by security. We told them that people from West Virginia were there to meet with their senator and find out why he hadn't introduced the compromise legislation that he'd told them about when we'd met previously. As the cameras from local media outlets surrounded us by the door, the security officer asked us to please wait outside. Several minutes passed before a member of Manchin's staff came out to tell us he was unavailable to meet because of his duties in Washington, D.C. Pam asked the staffer to please tell the senator that we'd see him there.

So, the next week, we went to Capitol Hill. Our organizers at Repairers of the Breach had reached out to folks across the country and shared our strategy to "March on Manchin" as a way of launching a season of direct action that would clarify the cost of compromise at this critical moment in our nation's history. Reporters asked, "Do you really think you can persuade Manchin and Sinema to change their position on the filibuster?"

"I can tell you this much," I replied. "We won't move them by carrying on with business as usual. They're not going to change just by meeting with us. They've already shown us that. But if we can expose how extreme they're being . . . if we can show the nation the people who are dying because they've reneged on their promises, then maybe we can change the story you're telling. Maybe we can stop calling this extremism 'moderate.' If we do that, they'll eventually have to change their position."

At our rally in front of the Supreme Court, we gathered with COVID masks on, determined to find a way to break through the narrative that made blocking policies that an overwhelming majority of Americans support seem reasonable. This was just the sort of nonsense that poor people across the nation had told us was the main reason they didn't bother showing up for elections. We couldn't act like this was normal. Our people had traveled on buses and were here, ready to risk their health and put their own bodies on the line to make clear how extreme Machin's position really was.

I explained as clearly as I could why a Black preacher like

myself was standing with a white woman like Pam to challenge Manchin. He had not put his hand on the Bible and sworn to *moderately* support the Constitution. He never once said when he was running for office that, if he were elected, he would join Republicans in their interposition and nullification of legislation to protect Constitutional rights. We were not opposed to compromise on principle, but the possibility of compromise is based on a shared promise—that every American over eighteen years of age, born or naturalized in this nation, has a say in the final outcome by exercising their right to vote. Republicans had shown us that they had no desire to even debate how to defend that promise. They had capitulated to the lies of a former president who lost reelection. They had sided with the corporation-funded think tanks and the extremists in statehouses who pushed legislation to purge voters who had turned out in 2020. Six months after the Capitol was stormed by a mob that wanted to overturn the results of an election, Republicans were taking the side of the insurrectionists. "How," I asked, "can you compromise with that?"

We walked from the Supreme Court to Manchin's office building, filling the street with a crowd as diverse as our movement. We'd written our four demands on placards that people carried as they marched side-by-side: end the filibuster, pass the For the People Act, restore the Voting Rights Act, and raise the federal minimum wage to $15 an hour. These were not radical ideas. The Democrats who controlled the federal government had run on them just the year before. Now, the consensus on Capitol Hill was that none of these proposals was going anywhere. As we passed the United Methodist Building, which sits just north of the Supreme Court, I noticed that their sign out front echoed our simple message: VOTING RIGHTS IS A MORAL ISSUE.

As our line stretched out toward the Hart Senate Office Building, we sang, "Somebody's been stealing our voting rights, and it's gone on far too long." When we said "somebody's been stealing our wages" in the next verse, we knew we were singing about the same somebodies. They were the members of the Republican caucus who stood unified against these policies that would save the lives of poor people and low-wage workers. And they were also the moderates who were delaying action by holding out a false hope that some sort of compromise was more realistic than doing what they had told voters they would do if they elected them.

When we arrived outside Senator Manchin's office, his staff told us once again that he was unavailable to meet. Sister Pam was standing there with me, as we felt the summer heat rising from the asphalt. She'd ridden all night on a bus with other folks who couldn't afford to take a day off, but also didn't know how much longer they could survive on the wages they were earning. They'd bet their families' well-being on the hope of breaking through a rock that looked like it wouldn't move. So we decided we would wait right there in the street for Senator Manchin. The least he could do was come and explain himself to these folks who'd waited months for the compromise plan he'd told them he was working on.

Capitol police officers came to tell us we would have to move from the street or be arrested. We told them we understood they were doing their job. "We aren't here for an insurrection," I said to one of them. "We're trying to help bring about a resurrection."

As I stood there and watched people who'd risked everything to make their voices heard submit to arrest, I knew that our action did not make sense from a political realist's perspective, even if, over time, such actions might build toward a movement that could shift public opinion. The risk–reward ratio of this direct action wouldn't add up for most organizations that try to influence legislation on Capitol Hill. Then I looked again at the people taking nonviolent direct action—people I'd gotten to know in the communities where they struggle to survive every day—and I saw them from the prophet Isaiah's point of view.

The new song that people from the hollers of Kentucky and West Virginia were singing together had led a remnant to the nation's capital. No, we had not yet been able to elect a majority that would represent our moral fusion movement, but the first victory in any movement for change is when the people stand together and refuse to accept that the way things are is the way things have to be. A nonviolent army of poor people that refused to be divided by race was standing together and defying the tired old myths in our public life. Pam had said it was time to wake up the nation. I wasn't sure how long it would take, but I knew she was speaking as a prophet in our midst, pointing the way toward the possibility of a Third Reconstruction in our time.

In a nation that has known far too much unnecessary death, many people have experienced rejection because of how they were born or who they love. Some have felt rejection just because somebody thought they had to have someone to hate in order to feel good about themselves. Others have been rejected because of their income, their race, their faith, their lack of faith, or simply because somebody decided in their own ideology that they had a right—a false mandate—to demean someone else's God-given humanity. But in a genuine hillbilly rhapsody that echoed out of the hollers of Appalachia all the way to the streets of Capitol Hill, I could hear the sound of stones that the builders rejected coming together as the cornerstone of a new America.

I watched Pam put her hands behind her back for the officers to zip-tie them. Then I watched Rev. Jesse Jackson, who'd rushed to hold Dr. King when the assassin's bullet took him down in Memphis in 1968, do the same. Here were hands that had known different kinds of rejection, but they were hands joined together in a movement that knew a better unity was possible. When hands that once picked cotton join the hands of poor white people, Latinos, Asians, and Natives; when faith hands join labor hands, and gay hands join straight hands and trans hands—when all those hands that have experienced rejection get together, our togetherness can become an instrument of redemption.

Together, the rejected can teach us to sing again that "This land is your land, this land is my land."

Together we can ensure that hope, not hate, has the last word.

We don't have to settle for the compromises that politicians offer as Band-Aids to cover the flesh wounds that are draining the life out of poor people. Even if we're a remnant, a prophetic perspective allows us to see how a minority committed to do what is right has the power to show the masses what is possible.

Stirred up by the old myth's lies, a relatively small group of angry and disgruntled people, who do not represent the poor white folks I know, were nearly successful in their attempt to interrupt our democracy on January 6, 2021. But a much bigger and broader coalition of Americans, made up of people who've experienced rejection, keeps singing a better song. We are not an insurrection, but a resurrection—rising from the rejection of our past and present to offer ourselves as a cornerstone for the reconstruction that must begin by lifting the nation from the bottom.

I watched officers arrest Pam and Rev. Jackson and dozens of others who'd joined hands to say they would not leave the street until they could meet with Manchin. Then I stepped into the street to join them as we sang "Ain't Gonna Let Nobody Turn Me 'Round." I could feel the old song I'd grown up singing harmonize with the rhapsody that had connected me with this remnant. Hand-in-hand, we were determined to lead the nation to a future where all of our children can thrive.

Chapter 10

REDISCOVERING THE TIES THAT BIND US

WHEN I WAS GROWING UP, MY FATHER USED TO love to tell a story about my great-grandmother who was a Brooks before she married a Keyes, and later a James. All the Brooks side of her family, he recalled, would swap labor during harvest season with the Keyeses and Jameses and a white family, walking the dirt roads between our family farms to get to work wherever they were needed back in the 1930s and '40s. When the crops were ready to pick in one family's field, everyone who was old enough to work came together to get them in. Then, when another field was ready for harvest, the whole group would go there and harvest the crops for that family. Grandma Keyes didn't touch tobacco because she said it was a vice to smoke the dirty weed. But for every other crop, this was how she and most other families around Free Union, North Carolina, got their harvest in and survived as dirt farmers before the days of machine pickers.

During World War II, my father served in the U.S. Navy, which, under pressure, had finally integrated. When he came back home, everyone was out in the field, working together as they had all his life. It may not have been the first time he'd heard it, but after his time away, it was the first time he noticed a young white man in the field call his grandmother "Auntie." Later, when he was headed back to the house, Daddy said to his Grandma Keyes, "You know, you don't have to let that man talk to you like that?"

"Like what?" Grandma Keyes asked.

"Disrespectful like that, calling you 'Auntie,'" he intoned. Like many Black men who'd served in World War II, my father was determined not to accommodate himself to Jim Crow's ways after risking his life for democracy half a world away. "That's how the plantation owners used to talk to slaves," he said to his grandmother, getting worked up with his passion for justice. "You ain't got to take that from him."

But Grandma Keyes just laughed and said, "Child, that boy calls me Auntie because I *am* his aunt."

Daddy loved the story, I think, because he understood how it interrupts the assumptions we're tempted to make when we talk about inequity in American society. In truth, so many of these people were actually related. We can't work for justice in America without talking about race, but we do not need to make white people our enemy to challenge racism. In fact, we can't. Because race differentiates in order to divide, no one can be truly "anti-racist" without searching for the ties that bind us and building coalitions across all the lines that are drawn to pit us against one another.

Grandma Keyes knew people who'd been considered property under the law because of the color of their skin—Black folks who could have been killed simply for asserting their dignity as human beings. Harriet Jacobs, an enslaved women born a half century before Grandma Keyes, just across the Albemarle Sound in Edenton, North Carolina, wrote the story of how, when she refused the sexual advances of the man who considered her property, he threatened to sell her children away if she wouldn't succumb to his wishes. Instead, she hid in an attic space above her grandmother's house for seven long years before she was able to escape to freedom. This wasn't history to Grandma Keyes. She grew up around folks who knew Harriet Jacobs's people.

At the same time, she also knew Black people who had worked with their white neighbors, worshiped with them, fallen in love, and raised children together for generations. Black and white folks in our community of Free Union were proud of the fact that they weren't kin because plantation-owning men had raped our foremothers. We were family because free people of various hues had chosen one another as family and community, and they had built a life together.

Grandma Keyes laughed at Daddy's confusion when he got all riled up at her white nephew who called her "Auntie." She knew a fusion reality that was stronger than the old myth's lies.

Daddy loved to tell the story because he understood how important her wisdom was to the work of building the America that has never yet been. He knew that work entails rediscovering the ties that bind us because the real America is a fusion mixture of Black and white and everything in between.

Every movement that has worked to reconstruct America from its beginnings down to the present has built power for those who lack it, but Reconstruction has never only been about power for Black people. What is so frequently forgotten is that white Populists joined fusion coalitions after the Civil War because they recognized their shared interest with new Black Republican voters in a policy agenda that would tax the wealth that had been stored up in the Big Houses of the South to guarantee public goods to all people, regardless of race. My daddy passed down to me what Grandma Keyes had passed down to him: a memory that the fusion coalitions that brought Populists and free Blacks together more than 150 years ago were rooted in bonds of love and family, community and shared history that offer us a far better story than America's old myths.

For generations, the free labor that plantation owners were allowed to steal from enslaved people kept wages down for poor white workers as well. As historian Keri Leigh Merritt has argued in her book *Masterless Men*, the plight of poor whites and their unwillingness to enthusiastically back the Confederate cause contributed to the Union victory in the Civil War, so there is a long tradition of poor white people who could potentially be organized for systemic change. Beyond that, Merritt argues, "[B]lack emancipation freed poor white Southerners in a variety of ways." The Freedmen's Bureau hospitals that were established after the war to offer healthcare to the formerly enslaved also treated poor white people across the South, for example. Decades before any American politician would propose the possibility of universal healthcare, Reconstruction experimented with providing it to Black and white people in the postwar South—all because a fusion coalition of Black and white voters elected leaders who sought to reconstruct a political economy that worked for all people. The same was true for universal public education. When Reconstruction governments taxed plantation wealth to provide the education that their new constitutions guaranteed to formerly enslaved people, they also made education accessible to many poor whites for the first time.

This, too, is our Southern heritage, a heritage that has all too often been denied and erased in the past. When poor white folks across rural America fly the Confederate flag today, they often say it's about "heritage, not hate." But the old myths continue to mislead them about their true heritage. Most poor white Southerners aren't the heirs of plantation owners who sent hundreds of thousands to die in a fight to try to hold on to human beings as property. Their true heritage is with those who didn't want to fight, like the Red Strings in North Carolina who placed a scarlet ribbon on their windowsills, imitating Rahab in the biblical story of Jericho to signal to fellow Red Strings that they didn't support the war. The Red Strings were not alone. "If you added up the African Americans, the Unionists, the anti-Confederate rebels, the anti-war crowd and those who simply hated what the Confederacy did to their home state," my friend the Duke University historian Tim Tyson has written, "they might have outnumbered the hardcore Confederates."

After the Union victory, these dissenters were the white Populists and new Black Republicans who formed fusion coalitions in nine of the eleven former Confederate states. In the half century following the Civil War, they won total control of state government at some point in Tennessee, Virginia, and North Carolina and enacted transformative policies that made the South more equitable for Black and white people. The so-called "war on woke" isn't only suppressing Black Americans' history. It's silencing this story, too.

When I look back at American history and think about the strides we've made toward a more perfect union, I know that fusion is the heritage that offers us a better hope. When Americans have been able to reject the lies of the old myth and come together in significant ways, we have amended the flaws in our Constitution, checked the power of corporate greed, and taken action to make sure everyday people have what they need—living wages and the protections of a union, access to healthcare and affordable housing, equal protection under the law for minorities and recent immigrants. None of these fusion movements has been perfect, but they have always appealed to what Abraham Lincoln called the "better angels of our nature." Black and white leaders like Frederick Douglass and William Lloyd Garrison, Ida B. Wells and Mary White Ovington, Dr. King and Dorothy Day have appealed to the moral commitments of our constitutions and the values of our traditions to call fusion movements together. Mass movements are not made by leaders, though. They consist mostly of everyday people whose names are not in the history books—folks who know in their daily lives the ties that bind us together. Fusion movements are made up of folks like Grandma Keyes and her white cousins.

Grandma Keyes's life spanned the long reign of Jim Crow in the South, between the Supreme Court's *Plessy* v. *Ferguson* decision in 1896, which said "separate but equal" was a justification for a two-tiered society, and the *Brown* decision in 1954, which said a segregated public education system could not be equitable. During those six decades, interracial cooperation was illegal across the South and unheard of in much of the nation. Grandma Keyes could not sit down at a lunch counter and eat a sandwich when she went into town to do her shopping. Though they were kin folk, her white and Black nieces and nephews couldn't legally go see a movie together on Saturday night.

Relationships that could lead to fusion coalitions were forbidden, and racial segregation was policed by the lynch mob as well as the sheriff's deputies. Yet, despite all of that, Grandma Keyes laughed in the face of Jim Crow and kept the hope of moral fusion alive. She and millions like her honored the lived reality of fusion in their families and communities—in church houses and juke joints—and they held on to the hope that a better America was possible because they knew a higher law than even the U.S. Supreme Court could impose—a moral order in which the shared humanity they experienced could not be denied. This is the vision that made America's Second Reconstruction possible. It is the inheritance that was passed down to me. And it is the legacy we must reclaim if we are to become the America we aspire to be when we celebrate our nation's independence and promote democracy around the globe.

In 1900, just four years after the *Plessy* decision, the poet James Weldon Johnson, who would later become a leader in the NAACP, was asked to compose a poem for a celebration of President Lincoln's birthday in Johnson's hometown of Jacksonville, Florida. Thirty-five years after Lincoln's death, Black communities still honored the hope of Reconstruction by remembering the president who had, despite his flaws, signed the Emancipation Proclamation and promised the possibility of a multiracial democracy. Channeling the deliberations that would give birth to the NAACP and the wisdom of moral fusion, Johnson, with his brother the composer John Rosamond Johnson, ended up writing a hymn for a children's choir. "Lift Every Voice and Sing" set to music the longings for liberty and a true democracy that motivated the fusion organization–building of the early twentieth century. It anchored those yearnings in a moral narrative that acknowledged the power of evil but did not give up on the possibility of America. Johnson's hymn passed the guiding light of this wisdom to future generations, teaching them to sing the hope that had sustained their foreparents through "weary years" and "silent tears." It became an anthem for the NAACP and the broader movement to expand democracy in the Second Reconstruction. Yet it is often remembered today as the "Black National Anthem" when it is sung at the Super Bowl or a Juneteenth celebration. Rather than continuing as a hymn to help us sing a moral fusion vision for the way forward to a new America, "Lift Every Voice and Sing" is often reduced to a nationalist anthem.

To be true to myself and the traditions that have shaped me as a moral leader, I've had to reclaim this heritage. When I travel the back roads of Eastern Kentucky or march with sister Pam and her friends in West Virginia, I'm determined to lift every voice and sing the song that can mend our every flaw and help us reclaim the ties that bind us to one another. Yes, the fears that were stirred up to persuade white people to vote against the agenda of fusion coalitions after the First and Second Reconstructions are still with us. Though its slogans change, the lie is always the same: it says that if Black people gain something, white people will lose something. White folks have been told—whether directly or through dog whistles— that they're going to lose their women, lose their children, lose their heritage, lose their country, even lose their God. If government programs were available to Black people after the 1960s, white folks were told that the government was going to have to take their hard-earned money to pay for them. Meanwhile, since the 1980s, politicians have slashed taxes for the wealthiest Americans, and corporations have robbed them blind, leaving many in need of the same government programs that the old myths taught them to hate.

It's important for me to say Black people have also believed a flip side of this lie that can also cut us off from our fusion heritage. It says: you cannot trust anyone with white skin. Yes, you might need to use white people within the institutions of American life, but old wounds keep many Black folks from believing that their white neighbors can ever truly understand their pain. You might work with a white person, but you have to keep your guard up. What's best for Black people, this lie insists, is to invest in Black organizations that work for Black progress. Black elites in America today are especially susceptible to this lie. They understand that their power is based on a claim to represent Black issues, and they sometimes see an invitation to join fusion coalitions as a threat to that power.

Any wholesale embrace of an identity that was created to divide people, though, keeps Black people from building the kind of coalitions that can win a governing majority in American society. When Black civil rights groups claim voting rights as "their" issue, they miss the opportunity to connect with the women, students, immigrants, and poor white people who are also impacted by voter suppression tactics. I'm convinced this framing of voting rights as a "minority issue" made it possible for Democrats in 2021 and 2022 to do nothing to restore the Voting Rights Act or to expand access to the ballot, even as they controlled all three branches of the federal government. Civil rights organizations couldn't win the issue on their own, but the loss didn't only hurt Black people. It hurts us all.

In truth, many white liberals also buy into this flip side of the old myth's lie when they ignore the needs of poor white people.

University communities perform their commitment to racial justice by supporting Black organizations or celebrating Black leadership—especially during Black History Month. CEOs hire Diversity, Equity, and Inclusion officers and send their managerial staff to mandatory trainings to encourage diversity. Yet white liberals often ignore the cries of the poor white people who camp in the woods along their exit ramps or work for poverty wages preparing their food. I've been honored at university events all across America, but I've never been invited to a university-wide celebration of the service workers on campus who are unionizing to ensure living wages and access to healthcare for themselves and their families. When we are honest about racism in America, we have to tell the truth that the inequalities race has been used to justify do not only impact the so-called "minorities." Race has been used to create an economy that normalizes disregard for all poor people, and we play into its divisions whenever we fail to challenge the conditions that have allowed 66 million white Americans to become poor.

After I'd been working with poor white folks in West Virginia for a while, they told me that they learned a long time ago that miners never got a pay raise without somebody dying. It made me think about the victories of America's Second Reconstruction that we celebrate in the civil rights community. Could we have ever won the Civil Rights Act without the murder of James Chaney, Andrew Goodman, and Mickey Schwerner during Freedom Summer in Mississippi? Black and white people died together in that struggle. Would we have ever gotten the Voting Rights Act if the Klan hadn't brutally murdered Jimmy Lee Jackson, Viola Liuzzo, and James Reeb during the Selma campaign? At Brown Chapel AME Church, the spiritual center of the Selma campaign, these are the martyrs whose names are on the wall—Black and white together.

What does it say about us as a people that we are so often unwilling to even consider change until people die—and not just any people, but people we consider "like us"? Black folks were dying in the South for decades before some white people from the North came down and died with them, grabbing the nation's attention. Do we continue to allow 800 people a day to die from poverty in the richest nation in the history of the world because we've somehow been persuaded that poor people are not like us? It would be racist to suggest that America can only address poverty when we see that it is a plague killing white people. Still, I have chosen to challenge white poverty because I know it is immoral to let the old myths keep us divided while a crisis that impacts so many of us goes unaddressed.

In San Francisco's Tenderloin district, Glide Memorial Church sits on a hill where dozens of people who have nowhere else to call home have pitched tents and built makeshift structures out of tarps. For years the church has served a meal every day and tried to offer emergency assistance to folks facing the unnatural disaster of poverty. When I visited Glide a few years ago for a mass meeting with poor people from across California, I got out of the car to walk through these people's homes in order to get to the door of the church.

I noticed a white man sitting on the ground outside a tent wearing a pair of coveralls. He had a graying red beard, a furrowed brow, and eyes that were sunken back in his head. When I first saw him ahead of me on the sidewalk, surrounded by his earthly possessions, I wondered to myself what had happened. What was his story? Who had he been connected to before the threads of community became tattered and he was left with nowhere to live but the street?

I walk with a cane and have an arthritic condition that prevents me from moving quickly. It's been a thorn in my side for more than thirty years, but sometimes this disability forces me to slow down and see more than I might if I could hop out of a car and dash into the next event. As I made my way toward the entrance to the church building that evening, this man I had noticed as I was walking toward him looked up and called me by name.

"Reverend Barber," he said, "thanks for not forgetting us. We're with you."

I paused to shake his hand and look him in the eye. "We're in this struggle together," I assured him, and we had a few moments to talk. But the program had already begun inside the church, so I continued into the sanctuary, took my seat on the platform, and listened to the testimonies of people who've been directly impacted by America's inequities.

Two Black women went to the microphone together. "Our people face racist gerrymandering and mass incarceration," one of them said, "and we've come to say, 'No more!' "

"My family lost our home to foreclosure while the government was giving bailouts to the bank that took it," the other woman said. "My ancestors didn't come to this country because we wanted to. We were brought here in chains. But we are *here*," she insisted.

Another Black woman from Oakland stepped forward to share her story. "I grew up picking cotton and cutting grapes," she said, "and I wasn't allowed to drink from the same bucket as the white foreman in the field." A Latina woman followed her, explaining how she and many others still feel the denigration of racism in their daily fight to survive. She owned her own food service business, but she and her daughter had become homeless after the city forced them to leave an apartment that was infested with black mold. She had been paying $1,000 a month to stay there, but she couldn't find anything else available anywhere close to that rate.

As I listened, I knew that everything those women said was true. The poverty they were experiencing couldn't exist in a country like this without the old myths that racism passed down to us. The white brother who'd greeted me outside, however, kept breaking into my consciousness, like an alarm bell calling me to wake up. *"Thanks for not forgetting us,"* he'd said. To really grasp the scale of poverty in America, the nation needed to see him standing right alongside these sisters.

I was supposed to deliver the closing message that evening, but I couldn't now give the talk I'd prepared. I looked to the back of that packed sanctuary and saw folks who looked like the brother who had greeted me. They'd come in off the sidewalk that is their home, most of them white. I stepped out from behind the pulpit and asked if they would come up and join me on the platform. I needed to practice a little bit of what I preach.

"We've got to be real about what poverty looks like, y'all. We can't challenge the government to tell the truth and not tell the truth ourselves," I said. "And we preachers are as guilty as anybody. So many of us talk a lot about tithing, but not so much about the crisis of poverty."

I asked the people in that room to look at the faces of the people standing in front of them—to look and really see, all of us together. Yes, racism was at the heart of every one of my Black sisters' stories, I told them, but that didn't separate their experience from the white folks with whom they were now standing. It actually united them. I wasn't sure how that white brother living on the street in front of the church knew my name, but maybe it was for the same reason that another white man back in Free Union so many years ago had called Grandma Keyes "Auntie." In some fundamental sense, we were family. He knew that, and he had asked me to remember it too.

These ties that bind us as a nation are evident in almost every kindergarten classroom, shopping center, and an increasing number of family reunions across America. Demographers tell us that as soon as 2045, white people will be one among many minorities in this country. One in five marriages in America today is interracial. The truth is, fusion is our only future. We may be a nation whose politics are more polarized than ever, but people are coming together in all kinds of ways, even apart from the movement-building plans of our campaign or any other.

In the winter of 2022, I traveled to Buffalo, New York, at the invitation of Starbucks workers who had heard about Repairers of the Breach and moral fusion. They wanted to talk about how our experience resonated with theirs. We drove to a storefront where the workers had set up an office to coordinate union drives in the midst of the COVID-19 pandemic. These were not professional organizers. They were young people earning $30,000 a year who'd taken on a volunteer job to challenge one of the most powerful corporate names in America.

The young baristas leading the effort—white, Black, and Asian—made a straightforward case to their fellow workers: Starbucks cannot earn billions for its shareholders without the labor of people like them who take orders, learn the names of regulars, and serve them their drinks, just the way they like them. At the same time, workers cannot afford rent, utilities, and the basic costs of living on the wages they earn at many Starbucks stores. By forming a union, workers can leverage their collective power to negotiate better wages and safer working conditions. The combined pressures of growing inequality, pandemic constraints, and rapid inflation compelled these workers to take action together. It wasn't clear that any one thing had led them to this tipping point, but suddenly they were caught up in a movement bigger than themselves and their own personal stories. They became frontline organizers in a new wave of moral fusion movement building.

Like most corporations in America today, Starbucks did everything in its power to defend its stores against this rising tide of unionization. To combat the effort coordinated from this one little storefront in Buffalo, the company sent in nearly 100 managers to discourage workers from voting to unionize. Still, Starbucks lost. Workers at two stores in Buffalo voted to form a union. Store by store, others followed suit from Arizona to Virginia. Like the sit-in movement of 1960, when the direct action of students against segregated lunch counters in Greensboro, North Carolina, were suddenly replicated in scores of cities across the South, the organizing that had started in this little storefront in Buffalo rippled across the United States. By the end of 2022, more than 300 Starbucks stores would hold independent elections and vote to form a union.

After I'd listened to these young folks share their story, I thanked them for inviting us and told them what I'd been telling workers across the nation since the beginning of the pandemic.

"If a society calls you 'essential' and asks you to work on the frontlines during a pandemic, it is immoral to then treat you like you are expendable." I affirmed the solidarity they were building out of their own experience, and I told them about in-home care workers and Dollar General employees and fast-food workers I'd visited over the past few years who are doing the same thing.

Back at the very beginning of the pandemic, I told those workers that I'd gotten a call from my friend Mary Kay Henry, who leads the Service Employees International Union (SEIU), which represents more than two million service workers in the United States. A white sister, Mary Kay was elected by service workers of every race because she has a fire for justice in her bones and she won't let anything stop her from organizing to support workers. From the earliest days of the COVID shutdowns, she was talking to healthcare workers who were overwhelmed by the volume of sick patients, fighting on the frontlines to keep Americans alive, often without sufficient personal protective equipment or hazard pay.

When Mary Kay called, she said we needed to find a way for Americans to hear directly from these workers. So while most of the country was still in lockdown, we'd agreed to host weekly "Walk Out Wednesdays" online, where a virtual picket line lifted up the stories of frontline workers. Through the worst waves of the pandemic, I'd spent my Wednesdays listening to workers on Zoom at midday, then teaching Bible study to my church on Zoom in the evenings. The cries of the Israelites in Egypt echoed in those workers' testimonies, and the prophet Amos's cry for justice to "roll down like waters and righteousness like an ever-flowing stream" spoke to the moment. In the back and forth between the Zoom rooms, I'd watched the tributaries of many movements come together in ways I could not have imagined.

I told those Starbucks workers in Buffalo that they were another tributary, and I hoped they would keep standing together and know that, all across this nation, others like them were doing the same. I said a prayer for them as we were leaving town, then I asked our driver if we had time to go by and see Niagara Falls. I'd never seen it, and I wasn't sure when I might have the chance to get up that way again.

As we paused to take in one of America's natural wonders, I found a silence within the water's roar and took a deep breath to still my spirit. It is an astounding sight to see the collective force of a great watershed come together in one place. All of that water begins as raindrops and bubbling springs, tiny streams and tributaries. But when it comes together, it alters the landscape. And it impacts everything downstream from that great event.

As I stood there contemplating Niagara Falls, it occurred to me that a watershed is long. The Mississippi watershed stretches from this nation's northern border all the way to the Gulf of Mexico. You don't get a Niagara Falls every two miles. But every so often, all of that energy gets focused in one place. And it changes everything.

Reconstruction in the American South in the late 1860s and 1870s was such a watershed moment. No one knows all the springs of slave resistance and streams of abolitionist organizing that conjoined to bring about that moment, but when those forces came together, they gave birth to the Fourteenth Amendment and its promise of "equal protection under the law" that has informed every stride toward a more perfect union that we have experienced since then.

Montgomery, Alabama, which erupted in 1955 with a mass movement against Jim Crow segregation, was a watershed moment. Rosa Parks played her part, and Dr. King played his. But as Danielle McGuire shows in her book *At the Dark End of the Street,* many years of struggle—much of it Black women's resistance against sexual assault by white men—culminated in the Montgomery Bus Boycott. There were also labor and civil rights struggles that fed into that nonviolent Niagara Falls, setting off a chain of events that brought down Jim Crow and made a Second Reconstruction possible in America.

As I sat there contemplating Niagara Falls, I realized that we may well be living now in the watershed moment of a Third Reconstruction. A historic uprising for racial justice in America in 2020 was immediately followed by a wildcat strike for economic justice in 2022. In between, poor voters turned out as never before to vote for candidates who spoke to the issues that impact their everyday lives.

Yes, these are also dangerous times when the old myth's lies threaten to undermine democracy. You cannot behold the force of a watershed moment without recognizing its danger. But if all of that force can come together to push toward the promise of freedom and justice for all, then the tumultuous times we are living through have the potential to alter the landscape of human history and reconstruct a multiethnic democracy where everyone can thrive. With a sober eye to history, I knew there was no way to guarantee that outcome. But as I watched the seemingly still water on the horizon fall into a cascade of movement, I had to acknowledge another basic fact of nature: once you're caught up in a movement like this, there's no turning back.

All those years ago in Mitchell County, at a little church full of white people, I had the chance to talk in pastoral terms with a group of folks who'd realized that the old myths had led them to a dead end. They knew that the system wasn't working for them, and they could see through the lies of the politicians who told them that Black people or gay people or immigrants were their enemies. They needed a new community to belong to, and they needed an agenda they could pursue together with a new coalition of unlikely allies. I told them that night that I wasn't ready to march to the home of their Tea Party state representative. But I did more than invite them to sing the truth of "Blessed Be the Tie That Binds." I challenged them to join us for the Mountain Moral Monday rally we'd planned in downtown Asheville the next day.

The rest of that story is a reminder to me that you never know just when a watershed moment is going to come. After some morning planning meetings that next day, I was at the hotel getting ready when brother Frank Jones, who traveled with me often back then, came in to tell me we needed to get over to the rally site because there was a traffic jam downtown. "Oh, no," I said, still worried about the prospect of building a fusion coalition in Appalachia on short notice. "If there's been a wreck or something, we might not be able to get a crowd together by start time." Frank laughed at me and said, "Hurry up, Barber! There wasn't any accident. It's OUR PEOPLE blocking all the streets."

I hadn't yet realized how hungry so many people are for a moral fusion movement that can show them who we might yet become.

Ten thousand people—the vast majority of them white—rallied in downtown Asheville that Monday afternoon in August 2013. It was the largest mass demonstration in that mountain town's history. When I finally made it to the back of the stage, a local leader of the Tea Party met me at my vehicle and tried to start an argument in front of some members of the media. But a group of older white women who were on the program to sing got between me and the politician and told him in no uncertain terms that none of us was there to listen to him.

Since that afternoon in the mountains of my home state, I've had the chance to travel the hollers and back streets of America, as I've already described in some detail, meeting poor white people who are hungry for a better identity and movement that can show their nation and the world who we might yet be. No doubt, there are millions of people who oppose them, and the networks funded by some of the richest people in the world will continue to amplify their voices. While those people are our opposition, they are not our enemies. Driven by myths that, in the end, will cut them off from the people they love most and from the things we all need to survive and thrive, they also need a better story. When we organize to build a coalition that can defeat them politically, we do it for their sake too.

In recent years, my friend Willie Nelson has brought his beat-up old guitar and joined the Poor People's Campaign at rallies to sing his song, "If you don't like who's in there, vote 'em out." I appreciate his good humor and practical realism when it comes to politics. But his insight is even more profound in a song he sings on a new album he released when he was 89. After grappling with the overwhelming challenges we face and the fact that some people are dead-set against the sort of movement-building we need to make real change possible, Willie sings:

> There are those who are blind so we'll all have to
> lead them
> It's everyone's job till we get the work done.

In the biblical imagination that I've spent my life cultivating, this is the notion of a remnant. When the prophets decry the evils of political leaders and cultural systems that prop them up, they always tell the people that God doesn't need everyone to stand up against injustice. God needs a remnant, just a small number. If a community will come together to declare that another way is possible, they can change the conversation in a society. If even a small group bears witness to the fact that the way things are is not the way things have to be, then everyone who is dissatisfied and questioning their circumstances has somewhere to look for an alternative.

As a preacher, I've learned from the poor people who are forming a remnant to reconstruct democracy today what the prophets were talking about thousands of years ago. That night back in Cleveland, when Teri shared her fantasy that, one day, we might all get together to challenge the lies that keep us apart, I had planned to preach the famous passage from Amos 5 that ends with the prophet's call to "let justice roll down like waters and righteousness like an everflowing stream." But until I'd read the prophet's vision again through Teri's eyes, I had never noticed how the cascade of justice that Amos foretold depended on the people in Amos's day doing what poor people are doing now: remembering the ties that bind them by coming together as a remnant calling for change.

In her work on social movements, Harvard University's Erica Chenoweth calls this phenomenon the "3.5 percent rule." After studying people's movements across the globe in different cultural contexts and at different moments in history, Chenoweth has concluded that a social movement that wins the active support of around 3.5 percent of a society's population wins its demands. The prospect of organizing a hundred million voters into a moral fusion movement in the United States is daunting, but it turns out that the movement itself doesn't need to be anywhere near that size. Because movements move people far beyond their immediate reach. By accelerating the active engagement of a relatively small portion of the population, a moral fusion movement can change the political possibilities for everyone.

So, while I am sober about the forces opposing democracy and an economy that works for all of us, I remain hopeful. From the Forward Together Moral Movement in North Carolina to the Poor People's Campaign that is now mobilizing poor people in almost every state, I have had a chance to walk with leaders like Pam and Stanley, Lakin and Sarah, refusing to be divided by the old myth's lies. In June 2022, they and many others mobilized tens of thousands of people for a march down Pennsylvania Avenue and a Mass Poor People's and Low-Wage Workers' Assembly at the base of Capitol Hill. For 100 minutes, poor people had a platform in the nation's capital to speak directly to the issues that impact their lives. I stood on the stage with Rev. Bernice King, the daughter of Dr. Martin Luther King Jr. and Coretta Scott King, looking across a sea of people that stretched as far as the eye could see. "This is what Mama and Daddy and so many others were working for," Bernice said to me. Together, we are remembering the ties that bind us.

And we are not alone. Low-wage worker movements like the one I've described at Starbucks continue to grow and have built strong, fusion leadership, insisting that living wages are a moral issue. The anti-racist organizing of the past decade has put a multicolor coalition on the streets and in polling places across the nation, electing a Congress that looks more like our communities than at any time in American history. Young people fighting for climate action and gun control recognize the need for fusion coalitions, and they are building deep and wide in the fight for their lives. Yes, reactionary extremism and white Christian nationalism are bolder and more visible than most of us have seen in our lifetimes. But as they used to say in South Africa during the struggle against apartheid, "only a dying mule kicks the hardest." They wouldn't be fighting us this hard if they didn't know we have the power to win.

So I take solace these days in a phenomenon in physics called Bernoulli's principle. It explains how wind pushes the wings of an airplane up by going faster over the top of a wing than it goes over the bottom, creating a lift. Because of Bernoulli's principle, a modern sailboat can sail against the prevailing wind.

When you're sailing downwind, everybody knows that the wind is pushing your boat. But Bernoulli's principle explains how it is possible to go upwind.

If the sail on a boat is set right, then the headwind has to separate into two flows: one flow goes around the sail from the outside, the other goes through the inside. The path of these two flows does not have the same length, but the two flows must arrive at the same time. This means that the flow outside the sail must be faster than the flow from the inside. By accelerating outside, this flow creates a vacuum that sucks up the sail. And it pulls the boat forward, into the headwind.

For a movement to succeed, it doesn't have to change the wind. It just has to gather a force that accelerates forward to create a vacuum that can pull the whole society forward. It's a sort of social Bernoulli's principle. If we set our sails right, then moral fusion can pull us where we need to go, even against the headwinds of injustice. We don't have to deny the headwinds; we need not pretend that the dangers roaring about us are not real. To hold on to hope that a Third Reconstruction is yet possible, we simply have to allow ourselves to be caught up in the moral fusion movement that is accelerating toward love, justice, and mercy for all. We only have to press on, forward together, and the power of our movement will create a vacuum that pulls the ship of state forward toward a Third Reconstruction.

HOW BLACK POWER SAVED
MY WHITE GRANNIES

Jonathan Wilson-Hartgrove

*Jonathan Wilson-Hartgrove greets children at a migrant
shelter on the United States–Mexico border.*

S OME OF MY FONDEST MEMORIES OF CHILDHOOD
are of long afternoons bouncing back and forth between
my great-grannies' apartments. Granny Bern, who rubbed lipstick on her cheeks and kept a large and busty photo of herself
at sixteen by her bed, lived one building over from Granny Taylor, a quiet ex-preacher's wife who dipped snuff and gave us
cocoa mixed with sugar when we asked if we could try some.
Each of my grannies had the same galley kitchen off a small
living room, with a single bedroom through a door beside their
TV. Granny Taylor's apartment smelled like fried chicken and
homemade biscuits, which sat covered on her stovetop every
Sunday after church when she cooked enough for whoever
might stop in to visit. Sunday's biscuits became bread pudding
later in the week, and her standard greeting was, "Y'all come
on in here and get something to eat." Granny Bern wasn't much
of a cook, but she always welcomed us with bright-red lipstick
kisses on our cheeks and an invitation to see what we could
find in her candy dish. If our parents were busy with work or
errands in town, my brother and I were little kings on holiday
at our country estate when we got to spend the afternoon at our
grannies' apartment complex.

Granny Bern had led the singing at her Baptist church for decades and was always happy to start a hymn whenever two or more were gathered in her living room. Granny Taylor had been married to a Baptist preacher for fifty years, but his untreated mental illness became more than she could bear in her seventies, after the children and the grandchildren were grown. She'd never had a driving license, so she walked away one day with nothing more than she could carry in a purse and, after staying with our family for a few years, made her home at the apartment complex, across from Granny Bern.

When it was too hot or cold or rainy to play outside, I loved to sit in one or the other granny's living room—I usually went the opposite direction from my older brother, eager for the undivided attention—and I'd ask them about what their lives had been like when they were kids. Granny Taylor would retell stories about going down to the spring box to fetch milk out of the cold water and carrying two chickens to town, one under each arm, with explicit directions from her mother about exactly what she should trade them for in order to feed the dozen mouths on their farm in Southwest Virginia. When she got a little older, during the Great Depression, Granny and her sisters were hired out as domestic help for well-to-do families in town. On the weekends, they took their earnings home and gave them to their parents, who did everything they could to hold on to the land they farmed until they couldn't anymore.

Granny Bern's memories of childhood weren't as vivid, but she remembered well her routine as an adult in the textile mill, where she stood every day to mark out patterns on the cloth for the next person down the line to cut, a single step in the process that gave us the clothes we still wore from the factory's discount store. After her husband died when their two children were young, Granny Bern had made ends meet with hard work and the help of family. I didn't realize it at the time, but when my grannies told me their stories, they were telling me stories of white poverty.

This was the 1980s in small-town North Carolina. We celebrated Martin Luther King Jr. Day at our elementary school, President Reagan told Mr. Gorbachev to tear down his wall, and our white Sunday School teachers taught us not to see color. "Red and yellow, black and white / all are precious in His sight," we sang, never pausing to ask why we didn't see anyone in the church house whose skin wasn't as pale as ours. On the state highway outside our town, I later learned, a sign was posted until I was six years old that warned African Americans not to linger after dark if they valued their lives.

If anyone had asked, we knew we were neither racist nor poor. Yes, the South had a troubled history and times had been tough for folks who never had much, but my grannies understood themselves to be blessed. And they were. They had lived to see their children's grandchildren play in the parking lot outside their apartments, and they had everything they needed— even some extra to treat the little boys who loved nothing more than an afternoon in their care. They and the community that raised us wanted me to understand that God had been good to us, that we were blessed to be living in America at the end of the twentieth century, and that we had a responsibility to share the blessings of our way of life with those who were "less fortunate."

What I didn't realize at the time and couldn't see until I'd learned the history of moral fusion politics from Rev. Barber was that the blessed world I enjoyed at my grannies' apartment complex was partly the product of federal policies made possible by the political engagement of Black Americans. The apartment complex that was my childhood playground was a Housing and Urban Development (HUD) community for senior citizens, and much of the food Granny Taylor shared with us was paid for by the Supplemental Nutrition Assistance Program (SNAP). Only looking back, after they had both crossed over the divide from this life, did I begin to understand how the life my grannies shared with me as a boy was sustained by government programs that many people in our community didn't support.

Since Jimmy Carter's campaign for president in 1976, a Democrat hasn't won a majority of votes for president in my home county. Backing Ronald Reagan in 1980, the New Right rallied white conservatives with talk about traditional and family values while they pushed a policy agenda that benefited corporations and slashed government programs that had lifted millions of people out of poverty. In a place where race had shaped identity for generations, the public appeals of this movement were no longer explicitly racist. Reagan made Martin Luther King Jr. Day a federal holiday and, at the same time, worked to undermine the federal antipoverty programs that King was working to expand through the Poor People's Campaign when he was gunned down in 1968. In the name of our values—and in ways that often suggested immorality among "those people"—we were invited to sell out the most vulnerable among us.

But Black people in other places, voting along with white progressives and other political allies, consistently fought to maintain the antipoverty programs that Republicans worked to cut and defund. Yes, my grannies were blessed—by God *and* by the political coalition that gave them homes at the end of their lives. If you'd asked either of them, Granny Bern and Granny Taylor would have told you that Jesus saved them. But the truth is that Black political power did, too. The HUD program, developed during President Lyndon Johnson's War on Poverty, expanded federally subsidized housing and gave my grannies a quality of life in their later years that allowed them to dote on the boys born to their children's children. The deacons at our local church taught us to "honor our father and mother," but the lesson they lived was "do as I say, not as I do." Whenever they went to the polls, most of them voted to sell our grannies out to tax breaks and talk of "economic growth."

When pundits observe the total control political extremists hold over government in places like the town where I grew up, they often wonder aloud how so many people have been persuaded to vote against their own interests. But this question, however sincere, doesn't capture the human tragedy of people coming to believe that selling out their grannies *is* in their best interest—a price they're willing to pay for the future they think they want. As Rev. Barber has helped me to see, the people whose votes determine the outcomes in America's so-called "red counties" are not, in fact, overwhelmingly poor. Many of them are the children and grandchildren—the neighbors and landlords—of poor white people who have too often had no champion in American public life. They are people who have believed the lie that they made their own wealth all by themselves. Their interest is maintaining an economy that has worked for them, even if it doesn't work so well for the people around them.

More than a decade ago—long before Donald Trump

stepped into U.S. politics—I visited with a civil rights veteran in Mississippi who has devoted his life to economic development in his home state. We were talking about the legacy of the Civil Rights movement in economic empowerment programs and community development initiatives that continued long after the more highly publicized desegregation campaigns of the 1960s. But this Black elder in his eighties—a man who'd been tortured by white officers in a Mississippi jail fifty years earlier—wept when he reflected on the poor white Mississippians he'd worked with over the years. "We had Dr. King and Malcolm," he said. "We had Medgar Evers and Ms. Fannie Lou Hamer as our champions here in Mississippi. But those poor white folk—they ain't never had a champion." His grief was genuine, and I realized as I watched the tears flow down his creased cheeks that he was crying for my grannies in a way that I had never been able to.

Grief breaks us all, but there is always the possibility that it can break us open—that it can, however painful, show us the way to new life. As a pastor, Rev. Barber understands that part of the malady of our common life in America is our failure to grieve. Rather than face the pain of loss, we have kept going by plunging ahead, holding on to hope that our best days are yet to come and running like hell from any evidence to the contrary. *White Poverty* then is an invitation to people who've begun to suspect that this mode of evasion is insufficient for the challenges before us. Another world is possible—but only if we are willing to face our pain and let it break us open.

Yara Allen, the song leader who accompanied Rev. Barber on that first trip to Mitchell County back in 2013, went with him a couple of years later to support a movement for environmental justice in my home county. At a Missionary Baptist church one town over from where I grew up, Yara listened to Black and white families tell similar stories about the strange symptoms their loved ones had experienced after the local utility started storing coal ash in ponds that leached toxins into the groundwater. Their sharing that evening became a memorial service that the community had not been able to have, and families that hadn't known one another wept together as they grieved the unnecessary death of mothers and brothers, children and friends. As she listened to their mourning, Yara wrote a song that she invited the congregation to sing with her.

Somebody's been hurting my people,
And it's gone on far too long.
I tell you, it's gone on far too long.
Oh I tell you, it's gone on far too long.
Somebody's been hurting my people,
And it's gone on far too long.
And we won't be silent anymore.

As a part of the Poor People's Campaign, I've had the opportunity to sing that song with poor and hurting people from every corner of this country. But somehow, from among the great cloud of witnesses, I always hear my Granny Bern's voice singing out above the crowd, like she used to from the recliner in her living room. And I know that people like her do have a champion in a movement that won't shut up until America faces our exceptional poverty and does right by the people who built this nation and keep it running every day.

ACKNOWLEDGMENTS

I N MY FAITH TRADITION, WE ALWAYS SAID, NO MAT-
ter how much we had or didn't have,

"Giving honor to God,
the Author and Finisher of my faith,
who keeps me clothed and in my right mind,
saved my soul,
gave me a reasonable portion of health and strength,
watches over me when I lie down at night in the posi-
  tion of death,
touches me every morning with a finger of love,
woke me up and allowed my golden days to roll on,
that I might serve by God's grace
and my living not be in vain."

If you've read this far, you know how indebted I am to my
mother and father, Eleanor and William J. Barber, who passed
the wisdom of moral fusion down to me along with the geneal-
ogy that roots my identity and reminds me of the possibilities
that are present in the ties that bind us across the dividing lines

of race in America. I thank them along with my family, who have prayed and stood with me and shared this work.

By now you know how moved I have been by some of the people who've shown me how white poverty exposes America's old myths and compels us to face our exceptional poverty. So first and foremost, I want to acknowledge all the people—many of whose stories I didn't have time to tell—who inspire me with their hope and tenacity as they face policies that are vicious and deadly. This book is dedicated to each poor person who has refused to believe what this nation's myths say about them and has dared to assert that they have an equal claim to the tools of their government and the promises of this democracy. You made this book possible, and you give me hope that a Third Reconstruction may yet be realized. To each of you, I say, "Forward together! Not one step back!"

To my many teachers from North Carolina Central University and Duke Divinity School whose wisdom guides me as I face the challenges of each day, especially those who spent extra time and saw things in me I didn't see: your lessons reverberate in my spirit.

My sincere thanks to all of the scholars whose work I've footnoted and to the think tanks and political leaders who have helped me make the case for moral public policy, especially the Institute for Policy Studies; the Economic Policy Institute; Columbia University's Center for Sustainable Development; and members of Congress who continue to push for the policies that a Third Reconstruction requires.

Thank you to Drew University for allowing me to do doctoral studies in public policy and pastoral care—reflection that has shaped my life's work.

I'm grateful to all who've had any part in me now being at Yale Divinity School, where I have the opportunity to pass the tradition of moral fusion movements on to incredibly gifted students through the Center for Public Theology and Public Policy—especially to our team: Valerie Eguavoen, Roz Pelles, and Jonathan Wilson-Hartgrove.

My sincere thanks to all of the staff of Repairers of the Breach: to those who we send to organize in the field; to those who sing; to those who secure the movement; to those who serve as advisors; to those who shuffle the papers and make administrative processes strong; to those who stretch themselves to make sure I can go and be in places where I would never be able to go without their help; thank you, all. And thank you to every person who has supported Repairers in any way to sustain this work.

Thank you to all who serve with us in the Poor People's Campaign, from our partners at the Kairos Center to every partner organization, no matter how big or small. "We" is indeed the most important word in the justice vocabulary, and I am continually encouraged by our "we."

Charlotte Sheedy, who was first introduced to me by my friend Tim Tyson, knows how books are made and what they can do in the world. She has been a literary angel, introducing us to the team at Norton and, especially, to Bob Weil, whose passion for this project was matched only by his skill at shaping it for the purposes we hope it will serve. The success of those aims is beyond the capacity of any of our individual efforts to determine, but if the goal is a democracy in which everyone can thrive and in which the means of moral fusion are now clear, then we have Bob and his excellent team to thank.

Jonathan is my brother and told me I had this book inside me. I thank him for helping me get it out.

If this book can serve to help build a movement to reconstruct democracy in America, then I will also have you to thank.

Rebuilding, Redemption & Revival Can Be Real

Inaugural Sermon for Joseph R. Biden

*Homily delivered January 21, 2021, at the Inaugural Interfaith
Prayer Service for President Joseph R. Biden and Vice President
Kamala Harris, hosted by the Washington National Cathedral.*

LORD, PLEASE HELP, HOLD, AND HARNESS US FOR
Your purposes and for Your glory. Amen.

Our text this morning comes from the prophet Isaiah,
chapter 58:

> *This is the kind of fast day I'm after:*
> *to break the chains of injustice,*
> *get rid of exploitation in the workplace,*
> *free the oppressed,*
> *cancel debts.*
> *What I'm interested in seeing you do is:*
> *sharing your food with the hungry,*
> *inviting the homeless poor into your homes,*
> *putting clothes on the shivering ill-clad,*
> *being available to your own families.*
> *Do this and the lights will turn on,*

and your lives will turn around at once.
Your righteousness will pave your way.
  The God of glory will secure your passage.
Then when you pray, God will answer.
  You'll call out for help and I'll say, "Here I am."
If you get rid of unfair practices,
  quit blaming victims,
  quit gossiping about other people's sins,
If you are generous with the hungry
  and start giving yourselves to the down-and-out,
Your lives will begin to glow in the darkness,
  your shadowed lives will be bathed in sunlight.
I will always show you where to go.
  I'll give you a full life in the emptiest of places—
firm muscles, strong bones.
You'll be like a well-watered garden,
  a gurgling spring that never runs dry.
You'll use the old rubble of past lives to build anew,
  rebuild the foundations from out of your past.
You'll be known as those who can fix anything,
  restore old ruins, rebuild and renovate,
  make the community livable again.

I take my text this morning from the prophet Isaiah. But the prophet, being able to see the future, may have taken his text from the old chitlin' circuit comic Moms Mabley, who used to tell what one strawberry said to the other strawberry: "If we hadn't been in that bed together, we wouldn't be in this jam today."

Well, we are in a jam today. Trouble is real, and whether we like it or not, we are in this mess together as a nation.

When this word of the Lord came to Isaiah, his people were also in a jam. Bad leadership, greed, and injustice had led them into trouble, exile, and economic hardship.

In that day, some tried to simply cover up the trouble with false religion and deceit. But God said to the prophet, "Sound the trumpet. Tell the nation of its sin. Tell them that just going through the motions of prayer will not get them out of this jam. I need them to fast from wrongdoing. I need them to repent of what got them here and turn in a new direction."

The prophet was saying then what Franklin Delano Roosevelt said in the 1930s to an America with "one-third of a nation ill-housed, ill-clad, and ill-nourished," besieged by the Great Depression and beset by bigotry and hatred. At such a time as this, FDR said:

"The rest of our progress is not whether we add more to the abundance of those who have much; it is whether we provide enough for those who have too little."

Isaiah was saying what Dr. King said to America when we faced a jam in the 1960s:

"The time has come for an all-out world war against poverty. The rich nations must use their vast resources of wealth to develop the underdeveloped, school the unschooled, and feed the unfed. Ultimately a great nation is a compassionate nation."

The prophet's basic question to the leadership of his day was the question the economist Joseph Stiglitz has asked: not how much will it cost the government to address inequality, but how much has it cost us not to?

It is the truth Aretha Franklin pointed to when she sang,

We have got to come together
We can rock this earth's foundation . . .

And so the prophet gives the nation God's clear guidance out of the jam it is in. First, repent of the sin. Then, repair the breach.

The breach, according to the imagery of Isaiah, is when there is a gap in the nation between what is and how God wants things to be.

Transposed to our time, the breach is when we say "one nation under God, indivisible" with our lips while we see the rich and the poor living in two very different Americas.

The breach would be knowing the only way to ensure domestic tranquility is to establish justice, but pretending we can address the nation's wounds with simplistic calls for unity.

The breach is lies when we need truth, greed when we need compassion, fighting one another when we need to find common ground, and hating when we ought to be loving.

And every now and then, a nation needs breach repairers to take us forward.

Mr. President, you have known the breach of economic struggle in your childhood and the breach of a broken heart.

Madame Vice President, you have known the political and social breach caused by the racism that tried to place a breach between the intelligence you had and the school you could attend. Your mother fought and organized because she knew this nation's breach.

And you both know that the only way forward is for breaches to be repaired.

This moment in our nation is not about left, right, or centrist. It should not be about Republicans and Democrats.

Even what we saw happen at the Capitol two weeks ago is the result of a long history—a politics of division that was cynically named "positive polarization" by those who thought they could use it for their own advantage. This strategy of feeding and seeding intentional division into the body politic spilled over into the inevitable violence that ideas of supremacy always produce.

If we want to come out of this jam and move forward together, we cannot accept the racial disparities, violence, and breaches that impact Black, brown, Native, and Asian Americans while offering collateral damage to our poor white brothers and sisters and ultimately our entire democracy.

We can't accept the poverty and low wealth of 140 million Americans before COVID and many more millions since.

These are breaches that must be addressed, and according to the text, repairing the breaches will bring revival.

"If you get rid of unfair practices," the prophet says.
If you are generous with the hungry
   and start giving yourselves to the down-and-out . . ."

Then "Your lives will begin to glow in the darkness . . ."

Then "You'll be known as repairers of the breach—
those who can fix anything,
   restore old ruins, rebuild and renovate,
   make the community livable again."

There is hope in the mourning.

Jurgen Moltmann once said:

"Faith, wherever it develops into hope, causes not rest but unrest, not patience but impatience ... Those who hope in Christ can no longer put up with reality as it is, but begin to suffer under it, to contradict it."

We don't have to put up with things as they are. We can contradict the breach with every prayer, every policy, every call to the people.

If we the people, with God's help, repair the breach, revival and renewal will come.

Weeping and mourning may endure in this night of our discontent, but joy will come in the mourning.

Love and light will burst through. God will hear our prayers if we do the work of repairing society's breach. No, America has never yet been all that she has hoped to be. But right here, right now, a Third Reconstruction is possible.

So let us ask God again what that great preacher and hymn writer Harry Emerson Fosdick asked in the midst of the Great Depression, when the nation was in a jam and needed some breach repairers ...

God of grace and God of glory,
on thy people pour thy power;
crown the ancient church's story;
bring its bud to glorious flower.

Cure thy children's warring madness,
bend our pride to thy control;
shame our wanton, selfish gladness,
rich in things and poor in soul.

Save us from weak resignation
to the evils we deplore;
let the search for thy salvation
be our glory evermore.
Oh God

Grant us wisdom, grant us courage,
for the facing of this hour,
for the facing of this hour.
Yes, God, grant us wisdom, grant us courage . . .

Until we make real the promise of liberty and justice for all.

Until thoughts of destroying one another give way to deeds of embracing each other.

Until our policies prove our promise of equal justice under law.

Until we decide too many have been hurting too long.

Until in every way we show in our democratic process that everybody has a right to live.

Until we lift from the bottom so that everybody rises.

Until the stones that the builder rejected become the chief cornerstone of a new social reality where, please God . . .

The poor are lifted
Sick are healed
Children protected
Civil rights and human rights never neglected
Love and justice are never rejected

Until there is racial justice
Economic justice

Living wage justice
Healthcare justice
Ecological justice
Disability justice
Justice for homeless
Justice for the poor and low-wealth, working poor
Immigrant justice
Until we study war no more and peace and justice are
the way we live

Until then . . .

God, grant us as a people
Grant us as an entire nation
Grant our president
Grant our vice president
Grant every preacher
Grant every politician

Grant every person, Black, white, Latino, Native, Asian, Jewish, Muslim, Christian, Hindu, of faith, not of faith but with a moral conscience, every human being created by God, documented or undocumented; gay, straight or trans, young or old . . .

From California to the Carolinas;
From Deep South Alabama to the hollers
of Appalachia;
From the Rio Grande of El Paso to the Potomac of D.C.;

From Georgia to the Great Lakes of Michigan;
From the farmlands of Kansas to the factories of
Pennsylvania . . .

Oh God, Grant us wisdom, grant us courage,
for the facing of this hour,
for the facing of this hour.

And one day, our children's children will call us what you have called us to be: repairers of the breach. Amen.

Notes

The personal stories I have shared here are based on my memory of experiences and my best effort to reconstruct the historical context in which they happened. For the past decade, Fusion Films has recorded much of the organizing work I have engaged in across the United States. Where footage exists, I have quoted directly from these recordings.

The following notes are offered to substantiate facts I have referenced in the text and to invite the reader into further engagement with the scholarship and reporting I've drawn upon in writing. My thanks to all the scholars and journalists whose work has informed my thinking about poverty, race, and inequality in America.

Preface

x   "Not everything that is faced": James Baldwin, "As Much Truth as One Can Bear," *New York Times Book Review*, January 14, 1962, p. 38.

xii   In 2016 there was *not a single county* in the United States: This is based on an analysis of housing data in the Institute for Policy Studies' 2018 report, "The Souls of Poor Folk: Auditing America 50 Years After the Poor People's Campaign Challenged Racism, Poverty, the War Economy/Militarism and Our National Morality," p. 10. Accessed July 12, 2023: https://www

.poorpeoplescampaign.org/wp-content/uploads/2019/12/PPC
-Audit-Full-410835a.pdf

xv   **the largest mass demonstrations for racial justice in our nation's history:** See analysis by Larry Buchanan, Quoctrung Bui, and Jugal K. Patel, "Black Lives Matter May Be the Largest Movement in U.S. History," *New York Times*, July 3, 2020.

Chapter 1
THE CRISIS WE CANNOT SEE

5   **"From the least to the greatest":** Jeremiah 6:13, New International Version.

6   **According to the federal government, nearly 40 million Americans:** For a calculator to see the threshold for any family size according to the OPM, see https://www.healthinformatics.dphe.state.co.us/NonAuthenticated/FPLCALC/

8   **Mollie Orshansky estimated that a family's budget was roughly three times the cost of what they spent on food:** For her own account of how she developed the formula for the OPM, see Mollie Orshansky, "Counting the Poor: Another Look at the Poverty Profile," *Social Security Administration Bulletin*, January 1965, p. 4.

8   **more than 19 million American renters are paying more than 30 percent of their limited incomes on housing:** This statistic, dating to 2022, accounts for the households that are technically "rent-burdened," according to the federal government's current measures. See https://www.census.gov/newsroom/press-releases/2022/renters-burdened-by-housing-costs.html

8   **600,000 people are homeless and millions more live on the edge of homelessness:** The U.S. Department for Housing and Urban Development publishes an annual estimate of people who are unhoused based on a point-in-time count conducted by local communities. These estimates do not include the "sheltered" homeless who live in temporary shelters or the millions of people

who live in their cars, "couch surf," or otherwise survive without any permanent dwelling. See the December 2022 report at https://www.hud.gov/press/press_releases_media_advisories/hud_no_22_253.

9 **Sixty-three percent of U.S. workers today live paycheck to paycheck:** See "New Reality Check: The Paycheck-to-Paycheck Report," Accessed July 14, 2023. https://www.pymnts.com/study/reality-check-paycheck-to-paycheck-consumer-planning-financial-emergency

9 **The average worker in America makes $54 a week less than they did 50 years ago, after adjusting for inflation:** See analysis by Drew DeSilver, "For Most U.S. Workers, Real Wages Have Barely Budged in Decades," August 7, 2018, Pew Research Center Report.

10 **The wealthiest 1 percent of Americans in 2023 owned more wealth:** See Federal Reserve data, https://www.federalreserve.gov/releases/z1/dataviz/dfa/distribute/table/#quarter:119;series:Net%20worth;demographic:income;population:all;units:levels.

10 **For a more accurate picture of poverty:** Because policy can only address the realities we measure, the fact that we dramatically undercount poverty in America limits our capacity to have serious policy debates about how to end poverty. The Poor People's Campaign argues that, in order to acknowledge the scale of the problem we face, the U.S. government must change its poverty measure. For further explanation of how we count 140 million poor and low-wealth people in America, see Shailly Gupta Barnes, "Explaining the 140 Million," https://kairoscenter.org/explaining-the-140-million/. These data were fact-checked by the *Washington Post* June 20, 2019, "Joe Biden's Claim that 'Almost Half' of Americans Live in Poverty," https://www.washingtonpost.com/politics/2019/06/20/joe-bidens-claim-that-almost-half-americans-live-poverty/.

11 **If you disaggregate the data on the 140 million Americans:** Disaggregating the data we have on poverty helps illuminate how the suffering created by inequality impacts every community. This

calculation of the impact of poverty on more white people, in raw numbers rather than percentage of the population, is based on an analysis of U.S. Census data that can be accessed here: https://www.census.gov/data/tables/time-series/demo/income -poverty/cps-pov/pov-01.html#par_textimage_10

12 **a report on America's peculiar exceptionalism of having the highest poverty rate among the world's major economies:** See Report of Special Rapporteur Philip Alston on his mission to the United States, 1–15 December 2017. Accessed July 17, 2023: https://digitallibrary.un.org/record/1629536?ln=en

13 **a Pew Research Center study of nearly 50,000 sermons:** Pew Research Center, December 16, 2019, "The Digital Pulpit: A Nationwide Analysis of Online Sermons."

13 **poor people from different backgrounds joined together in a Poor People's Campaign:** For a history of the Poor People's Campaign, see Sylvie Laurent, *King and the Other America* (Berkeley: University of California Press, 2019).

14 **"I must remind you that starving a child is violence":** Coretta Scott King, speech at Solidarity Day, Washington, D.C., June 19, 1968. The King Center, Atlanta.

15 **"the poor in white skins also suffer deprivation and the humiliation of poverty, if not color":** Martin Luther King Jr., "Remarks at the Convocation on Equal Justice Under Law of the NAACP Legal Defense and Educational Fund," Americana Hotel, Arlington, VA, May 28, 1964. The King Center, Atlanta.

Chapter 2
MORAL FUSION

17 **The summer of 2013:** I have written about the Forward Together Moral Movement and Moral Mondays in *The Third Reconstruction: Moral Mondays, Fusion Politics, and the Rise of a New Justice Movement* (Boston: Beacon Press, 2016).

21 **"from which cometh my help":** This is a quote from the King

James Version (KJV) translation of Psalm 121. Because of the KJV's influence on the biblical imagination in the English-speaking world, I quote its translation where that phrasing is well known to people in and beyond Christian communities. It is not, however, the translation I usually preach from. I have noted the particular translation I am referencing in other parts of the text for those who would like to consider the broader context of the biblical passage.

22 **During the brutal surge of vigilantism-turned terrorism:** An introduction to this historical context can be found in Cameron McWhirter, *Red Summer: The Summer of 1919 and the Awakening of Black America* (New York: Henry Holt, 2011).

24 **"the least of these":** This is a reference to the "Last Judgment" as recorded in Matthew's Gospel, chapter 25. Again, the memorable phrase here is from the King James Version (KJV).

24 **"Blessed Be the Tie":** This hymn was written in the eighteenth century by British hymn writer John Fawcett.

24 **"No one who has left home . . . will fail to receive many times as much":** See Luke 18:29, New International Version (NIV).

25 **"Loose the chains of injustice":** See Isaiah 58:6, New International Version (NIV).

26 **more than two thirds of the people in North Carolina who had been denied access to health insurance by the legislature's obstruction of Medicaid expansion were white:** The Health Access Coalition of the North Carolina Justice Center provided this analysis of the data at the time.

28 **"eleven o'clock on Sunday morning is one of the most segregated hours":** Martin Luther King Jr., from an interview on NBC's *Meet the Press*, April 17, 1960. Transcript available via Stanford University's Martin Luther King Institute: http://okra.stanford .edu/transcription/document_images/Vol05Scans/17Apr1960_ InterviewonMeetthePress.pdf

28 **"Which side are you on?":** Florence Reece wrote the song after her husband was arrested by Harlan County sheriff John Henry

Blair. Reece told the story in her book *Against the Current* (Knoxville, TN: Florence Reece, 1981).

31 **the words of Langston Hughes:** Langston Hughes, "Let America Be America Again" (1936).

33 *poverty abolitionists:* See Matthew Desmond, *Poverty, By America* (New York: Crown, 2023). Desmond's analysis makes an important shift away from those who suffer from poverty to the policies that sustain poverty. He argues compellingly that we need a new abolition movement to end poverty.

35 *"I'm pressing on that upward way":* Johnson Oatman Jr., "Higher Ground."

Chapter 3
PALE SKIN IS A SHARED INTEREST

40 **The *White Lion*, a Dutch warship with an English captain and crew:** For a critical introduction to the history of Virginia and the development of race summarized here, see James P. Horn, Peter C. Mancall, and Paul Musselwhite, eds., *Virginia 1619: Slavery and Freedom in the Making of English America* (Chapel Hill: University of North Carolina Press, 2019).

45 **In 1676, Virginia settlers, led by a man of European descent named Nathaniel Bacon:** See James D. Rice, *Tales from a Revolution: Bacon's Rebellion and the Transformation of Early America* (New York: Oxford University Press, 2012).

47 **a particular kind of social construction—a *historical* construction:** See Ira Berlin, *Many Thousands Gone: The First Two Centuries of Slavery in North America* (Cambridge, MA: Harvard University Press, 1998).

50 **"we made the world we're living in":** James Baldwin, "Notes for a Hypothetical Novel and Address," in *Nobody Knows My Name* (New York: Dial Press, 1961), 157.

53 **Formerly enslaved people became U.S. citizens:** W.E.B. DuBois

worked to recover the history of Reconstruction in his 1935 book *Black Reconstruction*, which challenged Columbia University's "Dunning School" and its acceptance of the Southern lie that Reconstruction had "failed." Columbia University's Eric Foner has dedicated his career to developing a historiography of Reconstruction that recognizes the key themes I've tried to summarize here. See Foner, *Reconstruction: America's Unfinished Revolution, 1863–1877* (New York: Harper & Row, 1988).

53 **"beneficent provision to the poor"**: North Carolina State Constitution, Article 11, Section 4.

54 **"enjoyment of the fruits of their own labor"**: North Carolina State Constitution, Article 1, Section 1.

54 **The experiment of the First Reconstruction, however, faced increasingly powerful and immoral opposition**: For a history of the nineteenth century's Redemption movement and the ways it twisted the moral narrative of Reconstruction, see Carole Emberton, *Beyond Reconstruction: Race, Violence, and the American South after the Civil War* (Chicago: University of Chicago Press, 2013). For contemporary analyses that trace the continuing themes of this history, see also Wesley Lowery, *American Whitelash: A Changing Nation and the Cost of Progress* (New York: Mariner Books: 2023), and Carol Anderson, *White Rage: The Unspoken Truth of Our Racial Divide* (New York: Bloomsbury: 2016).

56 **Thomas Dixon . . . offered a dramatic rendering of the myth in his 1905 novel *The Clansman***: Thomas Dixon, *The Clansman: A Historical Romance of the Ku Klux Klan* (New York: Doubleday, 1905). For a biography of Dixon and an analysis of his influence, see Michele K. Gillespie and Randal L. Hall, eds., *Thomas Dixon Jr. and the Birth of Modern America* (Baton Rouge, LA: LSU Press, 2009).

56 **"40 acres and a mule" promised to them by General William Tecumseh Sherman's field order**: Special Field Order No. 15, issued January 16, 1865, redistributed roughly 400,000 acres of confiscated land along the coast of South Carolina, Georgia, and

Florida in 40-acre plots to formerly enslaved people following Sherman's "March to the Sea." Later that year, following the assassination of President Abraham Lincoln, Andrew Johnson became president and rescinded the order. See Claude F. Oubre, *Forty Acres and a Mule: The Freedmen's Bureau and Black Land Ownership* (Baton Rouge, LA: LSU Press, 2012).

57 **In the decades following World War II, Blacks and whites, Latinos and young people came together and built organizational power:** Charles Payne's work in history and sociology of the Second Reconstruction has helped to highlight how a moral fusion movement was built by long-term organization-building at the local level. See Payne, *I've Got the Light of Freedom: The Organizing Tradition and the Mississippi Freedom Struggle* (Berkeley: University of California Press, 1995), as well as Jeanne Theoharis, *A More Beautiful and Terrible History: The Uses and Misuses of Civil Rights History* (Boston: Beacon Press, 2018).

58 **With the Second Reconstruction of the 1960s, America saw the desegregation of public schools:** For a history that puts the post–World War II freedom struggle in a Reconstruction framework, see Manning Marable, *Race, Reform, and Rebellion: The Second Reconstruction and Beyond in Black America, 1945–2006* (Jackson: University Press of Mississippi, 2007).

59 **In one of his last speeches, King said there's a schizophrenia in America:** Martin Luther King Jr., "The Other America," delivered March 14, 1968, at Grosse Pointe High School in Detroit, Michigan. In the last months of his life, King was captivated by the notion of "two Americas" that Michael Harrington had popularized in his book *The Other America: Poverty in the United States* (New York: Scribner's, 1962).

60 **The electoral attacks of this era were developed by Kevin Phillips:** For a good survey of this history, see Lisa McGirr, *Suburban Warriors: The Origins of the New American Right* (Princeton: Princeton University Press, 2001). For a helpful analysis of the way race and religion intersect in this period, see Anthea Butler, *White Evangelical Racism: The Politics of*

Morality in America (Chapel Hill: University of North Carolina Press, 2021).

60 **Republican strategist Lee Atwater later described how it worked:** From a 1981 interview with Alexander Lamis. Full audio of the interview was published in 2012 by *The Nation*. Accessed July 14, 2023. https://www.thenation.com/article/archive/exclusive-lee-atwaters-infamous-1981-interview-southern-strategy/

Chapter 4
ONLY BLACK FOLKS WANT CHANGE IN AMERICA

66 **"temporarily abled":** Reynolds Price, *A Whole New Life* (New York: Atheneum, 1994), p. 98.

66 **to instruct our elected representatives:** North Carolina State Constitution, Article 1, Section 12.

67 **The National Association for the Advancement of Colored People (NAACP) . . . was established in 1911 by white and Black Americans:** For a history of the NAACP, see Patricia Sullivan, *Lift Every Voice* (New York: New Press, 2010).

68 **Ida B. Wells . . . saw clearly how lynching was as much a fight about who America imagines itself to be as it was a struggle for political control:** For an account of Ida B. Wells's crusade against lynching and its context, see Paula J. Giddings, *Ida: A Sword Among Lions* (New York: Amistad, 2009).

70 **when Black and white organizers with the SNCC worked with local activists in Dallas County, Alabama:** For a history of the Selma Campaign and its role in America's Second Reconstruction, see Robert A. Pratt, *Selma's Bloody Sunday* (Baltimore: Johns Hopkins University Press, 2017).

71 **Dr. King gave one the most penetrating analyses ever offered in American public life:** Dr. Martin Luther King Jr., "Our God Is Marching On," delivered March 25, 1965. Full text available

from Stanford University's Martin Luther King, Jr. Institute. Accessed July 12, 2023. https://kinginstitute.stanford.edu/our -god-marching

73   According to the Pew Research Center, the median Black household income in 1967: See Pew Research Center data at: https:// www.pewresearch.org/social-trends/2016/06/27/1-demographic -trends-and-economic-well-being/

74   the ways we account for wealth distribution make America's crisis of poverty difficult to see: See Emmanuel Saez and Gabriel Zucman, "The Rise of Income and Wealth Inequality in America: Evidence from Distributional Macroeconomic Accounts." *The Journal of Economic Perspectives* 34, no. 4 (2020): 3.

76   Trump lost voters who made less than $50,000: See data at https:// www.statista.com/statistics/631244/voter-turnout-of-the-exit -polls-of-the-2016-elections-by-income/

Chapter 5
POVERTY IS ONLY A BLACK ISSUE

82   "Critical access" hospitals in America's rural communities: For a brief introduction to the history of rural hospitals and the Hill-Burton Act, see D. E. Newton, "Hill-Burton Act." In *The Gale Encyclopedia of Public Health* (2nd ed.), 2020.

83   a half million uninsured North Carolinians who were technically eligible for Medicaid still couldn't access health insurance: The Health Access Coalition of the North Carolina Justice Center provided this analysis of the data at the time.

86   Bob Zellner, a gregarious white man in his seventies at the time: Bob has shared his own story in a compelling memoir titled *The Wrong Side of Murder Creek* (Athens, GA: New South Books, 2008). In 2020, Spike Lee produced a film version of Bob's story titled *Son of the South*.

90   Emmett Till . . . was lynched: For a detailed account of Till's

life, his mother's response to his brutal murder, and the role she played in America's Second Reconstruction, see Tim Tyson, *The Blood of Emmett Till* (New York: Simon & Schuster, 2017).

93   **At the height of America's War on Poverty:** For a critical assessment of the War on Poverty, see Kyle Farmby, ed., *The War on Poverty: A Retrospective* (Minneapolis: Lexington Books/Fortress Academic, 2014).

94   **In 1936, Dorothea Lange . . . took her camera into a pea field:** For the story of Dorothea Lange's "Migrant Mother" series, see Winifred Fluck, "Poor Like Us: Poverty and Recognition in American Photography," *American Studies 55*, no. 1 (2010): 63–93.

95   **Ronald Reagan began citing the tale of a Black woman from Chicago:** See Josh Levin, *The Queen: The Forgotten Lie Behind an American Myth* (Boston: Little, Brown, 2019).

Chapter 6
WE CAN'T OVERCOME DIVISION

109   **Nancy MacLean . . . wrote a book called *Democracy in Chains*:** See Nancy MacLean, *Democracy in Chains: The Deep History of the Radical Right's Stealth Plan for America* (New York: Viking, 2017).

112   **Slaveholder religion used Scripture and moral reasoning to justify human bondage:** See Jonathan Wilson-Hartgrove, *Reconstructing the Gospel: Finding Freedom from Slaveholder Religion* (Downers Grove, IL: InterVarsity Press, 2018).

112   **"With ample funding from major corporations":** See Kevin Kruse, *One Nation Under God: How Corporate America Invented Christian America* (New York: Basic Books, 2015), xiv.

113   **reactionaries within the New Right understood that . . . they**

needed to organize white people around their religion rather than their race: For more on the networked organizations that created today's radical right, see Katherine Stewart, *The Power Worshippers: Inside the Dangerous Rise of Religious Nationalism* (New York: Bloomsbury, 2019). For an intellectual history of the Religious Right, see Randall Balmer, *Thy Kingdom Come: How the Religious Right Distorts the Faith and Threatens America* (New York: Basic Books, 2007).

113 A political operative named Paul Weyrich: For more on Weyrich and the role of the Council for National Policy, see Anne Nelson, *Shadow Network: Media, Money, and the Secret Hub of the Radical Right* (New York: Bloomsbury, 2019).

115 Sociologists in America today call people like that man who visited me "white Christian nationalists": See Samuel L. Perry and Andrew L. Whitehead, *Taking America Back for God: Christian Nationalism in the United States* (New York: Oxford University Press, 2020) as well as Philip S. Gorski and Samuel L. Perry, *The Flag and the Cross: White Christian Nationalism and the Threat to American Democracy* (New York: Oxford University Press, 2022). Robert Jones and the Political Religion Research Institute (PRRI) publish regular survey data on Christian nationalism and its influence on public issues in American life. See https://www.prri.org/research/a-christian-nation-understanding-the-threat-of-christian-nationalism-to-american-democracy-and-culture/

118 where President Lyndon Johnson went to launch the War on Poverty in 1964: See Pam Fessler, "Kentucky County That Gave War on Poverty a Face Still Struggles," January 8, 2014, National Public Radio. Accessed July 12, 2023: https://www.npr.org/2014/01/08/260151923/kentucky-county-that-gave-war-on-poverty-a-face-still-struggles

120 Our team . . . had created a set of slides: For more information on resources available from Repairers of the Breach, visit www.breachrepairers.org.

Chapter 7
FACING WHITE POVERTY'S WOUNDS

125 **Like Mitchell County, North Carolina, Corbin recruited Black men to work on the railroad:** See Elliot Jaspin, *Buried in the Bitter Waters: The Hidden History of Racial Cleansing in America* (New York: Basic Books, 2007). For more on the racial cleansing that happened in Corbin, see pages 167–83.

129 **The daily, ongoing traumatic stress that all poor people face:** For an overview of the research in psychology that had tried to understand how the persistent trauma of poverty impacts individuals' well-being, see Aviva Goral et al., "Development and Validation of the Continuous Traumatic Stress Response Scale (CTSR) Among Adults Exposed to Ongoing Security Threats," PLOS One 16, no. 6 (June 7, 2021).

134 **Poverty . . . is the fourth leading cause of death in America:** See David Brady et al., "Novel Estimates of Mortality Associated with Poverty in the US," *Journal of the American Medical Association Internal Medicine* 183, no. 6 (June 2023): 618–19.

136 **A study in 2017 found that only 3 percent of working-age adults were out of the labor market for unknown reasons:** See Jay Shambaugh et al., "Who Is Poor in the United States? Examining the Characteristics and Workforce Participation of Impoverished Americans." Brookings Institution, October 2017, 1–10. https://www.brookings.edu/wp-content/uploads/2016/07/who_is_poor_in_the_us-1.pdf.

137 **Frances Perkins . . . became America's first female labor secretary:** For a biography of Frances Perkins that highlights her moral influence on the New Deal, see Kirstin Downey, *The Woman Behind the New Deal: The Life of Frances Perkins, FDR's Secretary of Labor and His Moral Conscience* (New York: Doubleday, 2009).

137 **"No business which depends for its existence":** Franklin Delano Roosevelt, "Statement on the National Industrial Recovery Act," June 16, 1933. Franklin D. Roosevelt Presidential Library.

137 **agenda for the 1963 March on Washington . . . included union**

rights and a living wage of $2 an hour for all Americans: The
10 demands of the March on Washington were published in the
program for the event. For more on the story behind the organizing of the event and its policy agenda, see Julian Bond, *Julian
Bond's Time to Teach: A History of the Southern Civil Rights
Movement* (Boston: Beacon Press, 2021), 239–57.

138 fast-food jobs didn't disappear: David Card and Alan Krueger,
"Minimum Wages and Employment: A Case Study of the Fast-
Food Industry in New Jersey and Pennsylvania," *American Eco-
nomic Review* 84 (1994): 772–93.

138 "Woe to him who builds his palace by unrighteousness": Jeremiah 22:13, New International Version (NIV).

140 Throughout the 1950s and '60s . . . nearly a third of all U.S.
workers were union members: For history of the labor movement in the United States, see Kim Kelly, *Fight Like Hell: The
Untold History of American Labor* (New York: Atria, 2022);
and Philip Dray, *There Is Power in a Union: The Epic Story of
Labor in America* (New York: Anchor, 2011).

140 Anne Case and Angus Deaton have connected this decline in
economic well-being with an increase in morbidity: See Anne
Case and Angus Deaton, *Deaths of Despair and the Future of
Capitalism* (Princeton: Princeton University Press, 2022).

143 Since the Supreme Court's 2013 decision in *Shelby County v.
Holder*: For more on the struggle for voting rights, see Ari
Berman, *Give Us the Ballot: The Modern Struggle for Voting Rights in America* (New York: Farrar, Straus and Giroux:
2015), and Carol Anderson, *One Person, No Vote: How Voter
Suppression Is Destroying Democracy* (New York: Bloomsbury,
2018). See also Democracy Docket, an online resource Marc
Elias has created to update the public on legislation related to
voting rights: https://www.democracydocket.com; as well as the
Brennan Center for Justice, which tracks voter suppression bills
introduced in state legislatures: https://www.brennancenter
.org/issues/ensure-every-american-can-vote/voting-reform/
state-voting-laws

145 the court found that the law targeted African Americans with "almost surgical precision": "N.C. State Conference of the Naacp v. McCrory," 831 F.3d 204 (4th Cir. 2016). https://casetext.com/case/nc-state-conference-of-the-naacp-v-mccrory.

145 Whether or not they vote for politicians who champion these policies, poor white people benefit from expansions of democracy that lead to more progressive policies: See Gavin Wright, *Sharing the Prize: The Economics of the Civil Rights Revolution in the American South* (Cambridge, MA: Harvard University Press, 2018).

146 the more poor people are segregated in places with other poor people, the less they participate in local and national elections: See Amy Melissa Widestrom, "Impoverished Democracy: Economic Inequality, Residential Segregation, and the Decline of Political Participation" (2008). Syracuse University Libraries, Political Science: Dissertations. https://surface.syr.edu/psc_etd/9.

Chapter 8
POOR PEOPLE ARE THE NEW SWING VOTERS

150 "a conspiracy of her princes within her like a roaring lion tearing its prey": Ezekiel 22:25, New International Version. The subsequent quotes are also from Ezekiel 22. The valley of dry bones vision is found in Ezekiel 37.

153 Vance wrote about how his own life: See J. D. Vance, *Hillbilly Elegy: A Memoir of a Family and Culture in Crisis* (New York: HarperCollins, 2016).

154 Vance called himself a "never-Trump" conservative during the 2016 campaign: For reporting on Vance's criticism of Trump and later embrace, see Natalie Allison, " 'My god what an idiot': J. D. Vance Gets Whacked for Past Trump Comments," *Politico*, October 23, 2021. https://www.politico.com/news/2021/10/23/jd-vance-ohio-senate-trump-comments-516865

158 Nationwide, the 2018 midterms saw a roughly 10 percent increase in voter participation over the previous midterms: Data on participation of poor Americans is taken from a report by Robert Paul Hartley, "Unleashing the Power of Poor and Low-Income Americans," Poor People's Campaign, August 2020. https://www.poorpeoplescampaign.org/wp-content/uploads/2020/08/PPC-Voter-Research-Brief-18.pdf

159 Donald Trump won every income bracket above $50,000 by 1 to 4 points, but he lost every bracket below $50,000 by more than 9 points: See data at https://www.statista.com/statistics/631244/voter-turnout-of-the-exit-polls-of-the-2016-elections-by-income/.

162 With an overall turnout nearly 14 percentage points higher than four years earlier: Based on analysis of county-level voter data. See https://elect.ky.gov/Resources/Documents/voterturnoutcounty-2019G-20200323-080539.pdf.

163 "elections don't have to be about Right versus Left; they are still about right versus wrong": For video of Beshear's speech, see https://www.nytimes.com/video/us/elections/100000006810114/kentucky-election-bevin-beshear.html.

163 as high as 17 percent in the typical Democratic strongholds of Fayette and Jefferson counties: Based on analysis of county-level voter data. See https://elect.ky.gov/Resources/Documents/voterturnoutcounty-2019G-20200323-080539.pdf.

167 lower-income Americans died at as much as five times the rate: "A People's Pandemic Report," April 2022, p. 2. https://www.poorpeoplescampaign.org/wp-content/uploads/2022/04/ExecutiveSummary_7.pdf.

167 as many as 330,000 Americans died not simply from the disease, but because they lacked access to the healthcare they needed: See Alison Galvani et al., "Universal Healthcare As Pandemic Preparedness: The Lives and Costs that Could Have Been Saved During the COVID-19 Pandemic," *Proceedings of the National Academy of Sciences US*, June 13, 2022. https://www.pnas.org/doi/10.1073/pnas.2200536119.

168 "America, Accepting Death Is No Longer an Option": A recording of this sermon is available from the National Cathedral: https://youtu.be/eviTAayTGT4?si=P0z3rvM91_zHfXM4.

169 The prophet Amos promised that, if we would engage in a general lament: Amos 5, *The Message Bible* (MSG), translated by Eugene Peterson. Peterson, who was a Presbyterian pastor in suburban Maryland, said he wanted to go to Selma in 1965 when Dr. King called for the support of clergy, but the Lord told him to stay and challenge racism among the white people of suburbia. His translation of the prophets' original Hebrew into contemporary American English often captures the dramatic imagery of the prophetic imagination for our time.

171 "ending poverty will not just be an aspiration": See Jack Jenkins, "Biden Talks Faith and Poverty at Poor People's Campaign Event," Religion News Service, September 15, 2020. https://religionnews.com/2020/09/15/biden-talks-faith-and-poverty-at-poor-peoples-campaign-event/.

172 at least six million more low-income people had voted in 2020 than in 2016: Sarah Anderson and Margot Rathke, "After Boosting Low-Income Voter Turnout, Poor People's Campaign Mobilizes for Covid Relief," Inequality.org, November 9, 2020. https://inequality.org/great-divide/poor-peoples-campaign-voter-turnout/

172 Biden over Trump by as many as 15 percentage points: See exit poll data at https://www.statista.com/statistics/1184428/presidential-election-exit-polls-share-votes-income-us/.

172 In a state that Trump won, the measure passed: See news report at https://www.nytimes.com/interactive/2020/11/03/us/elections/results-florida-amendment-2-raise-minimum-wage.html.

Chapter 9
WHY WE MUST LIFT FROM THE BOTTOM

175 "repairer of the breach": Isaiah 58:12, King James Version.

178 more than 2.2 million people turned out in a special election

in Georgia to elect Rev. Dr. Raphael Warnock and Jon Ossoff: See Official Election Result of January 5, 2021, Federal Runoff Election, https://results.enr.clarityelections.com/GA/107556/web.274956/#/summary.

179   Manchin was suggesting that a higher minimum wage could hurt working people from his state: See reporting by Jordain Carney, "Manchin Says He Doesn't Support Raising Minimum Wage to $15 Per Hour," The Hill, February 2, 2021. https://thehill.com/homenews/senate/536977-machin-says-he-doesnt-support-raising-minimum-wage-to-15-per-hour/.

180   I was reminded of Dr. Martin Luther King Jr.'s reflection in his letter from the Birmingham City Jail: See Martin Luther King Jr., "Letter from Birmingham City Jail" (Philadelphia: American Friends Service Committee, May 1963). The letter was published in Ebony magazine later that summer and the following year in King's book, Why We Can't Wait.

182   Manchin . . . announced that he was also refusing to join the Democratic majority to override the Republican filibuster and pass the For the People Act: See reporting by Sahil Kapur et al., "Manchin, Sinema Join Senate GOP in Rejecting Filibuster Rule Change, Dooming Voting Bills," NBC News, January 19, 2022. https://www.nbcnews.com/politics/congress/democrats-voting-rights-bill-heads-toward-defeat-amid-gop-blockade-n1287685.

182   No single representative in American public life embodied the fight for voting rights more than John Lewis: For an introduction to John Lewis and his legacy of championing voting rights, see the film John Lewis: Good Trouble, by Erika Alexander, Dawn Porter, and Ben Arnon, Magnolia Home Entertainment, 2020.

183   more than 250 proposed changes to voting laws had been introduced by Republicans in state legislatures across the United States in the winter and spring of 2021: See voter suppression legislation tracker at the Brennan Center: https://www.brennancenter.org/issues/ensure-every-american-can-vote/voting-reform/state-voting-laws.

Chapter 10
Rediscovering the Ties that Bind Us

196   "[B]lack emancipation freed poor white Southerners": Keri Leigh Merritt, *Masterless Men: Poor Whites and Slavery in the Antebellum South* (New York: Cambridge University Press, 2017), 3.

197   **Red Strings in North Carolina:** See Scott Nelson, "Red Strings and Half-Brothers" in John C. Inscoe and Robert C. Kenzer, eds., *Enemies of the Country: New Perspectives on Unionists in the Civil War South* (Athens, GA: University of Georgia Press, 2004), 37–53.

197   **"If you added up":** Tim Tyson, *News and Observer*, August 17, 2017. https://www.newsobserver.com/opinion/op-ed/article31123988.html#storylink=cpy.

198   **"better angels of our nature":** Abraham Lincoln, "First Inaugural Address," March 4, 1861. https://www.gilderlehrman.org/sites/default/files/inline-pdfs/01264_0.pdf.

199   **a poem for a celebration of President Lincoln's birthday:** For the story of "Lift Every Voice and Sing," see Imani Perry, *May We Forever Stand: A History of the Black National Anthem* (Chapel Hill, NC: University of North Carolina Press, 2018).

206   **white people will be one among many minorities in this country:** For a summary report, see Stef W. Kight, "America's Majority Minority Future," https://www.axios.com/2019/04/29/when-american-minorities-become-the-majority.

207   **Starbucks did everything in its power:** For reporting on Starbucks union organizing and the corporation's resistance, see Rani Molla, "How a Bunch of Starbucks Baristas Built a Labor Movement," Vox.com, April 8, 2022. https://www.vox.com/recode/22993509/starbucks-successful-union-drive.

213   **Willie sings:** *"There are those who are blind so we'll all have to lead them . . .":* from "(We Are) The Cowboys," lyrics by Billy Joe Shaver. Recorded on the album *First Rose of Spring*, Legacy Records, July 3, 2020.

214　Erica Chenoweth calls this phenomenon the "3.5 percent rule": See Erica Chenoweth, *Civil Resistance: What Everyone Needs to Know* (New York: Oxford University Press, 2021).

Epilogue
HOW BLACK POWER SAVED MY WHITE GRANNIES

221　a sign was posted until I was six years old that warned African Americans not to linger after dark: For more on the history of "Sundown towns" in the United States, see James Loewen, *Sundown Towns: A Hidden Dimension of American Racism* (New Press, 2005).

222　the New Right rallied white conservatives: For more on this, see Jonathan Wilson-Hartgrove, *Revolution of Values: Reclaiming Public Faith for the Common Good* (InterVarsity Press, 2019).

INDEX

as historical construction, 47–48
Kentucky history of, 125–26
legal/political invention of, 39–47
North Carolina history of, 22–23
ongoing nature of, 73
as opportunity for learning, 149–50
poverty rates and, xiii–xiv, 11
power of, 35
Trump and, 102
voter suppression and, 143–44, 145
See also Black poverty myth; white shared interests myth
Randolph, A. Philip, 137
Reagan, Ronald, 61–62, 95, 222
Reconstruction. *See* First Reconstruction; Second Reconstruction; Third Reconstruction
Rednecks, xvii, 29
Red Strings, 197
Reeb, James, 202
Reece, Florence, 29, 244–45
religion-based myths
backlash against New Deal and, 112–13
Capitol insurrection and, 115–16
culture wars and, 113–15, 126–27
economic oppression policy and, 112–13, 114–15, 118–19, 120, 121
enslavement and, 43–45, 112
First Reconstruction backlash and, 112
Jim Crow and, 113
libertarianism and, 118–19
national divisions and, 98, 99–100
national divisions inevitability myth and, 112, 114–15
white shared interests myth and, 43–45
Religious Right, 113–14
remnant concept, 101, 190, 191, 212–14
Repairers of the Breach, 100–101, 103–4, 120–21, 177, 183–84, 187
See also minimum wage/voting rights campaign (2021)

Republican Party
blame of poor people and, 10
Capitol insurrection and, 188
COVID-19 pandemic and, 167
Medicaid expansion refusals and, 83
Repairers of the Breach and, 103
Southern Strategy, 60–62, 108, 109, 119–20
2020 federal election and, 177
voter suppression and, 183
Rolfe, John, 40
Roosevelt, Franklin D., 94, 137

Saez, Emmanuel, 74
Sanders, Bernie, 165
Schwerner, Mickey, 60, 202
Second Reconstruction, 57–60
backlash against, 60–62, 113, 222
cultures of fear and, 145–46, 200
economic justice and, 58–59, 110, 145, 222, 224
fusion movements and, 57–60, 68, 70–71, 87–88, 149, 247
"Lift Every Voice and Sing" and, 199–200
War on Poverty, 58–59, 93, 94–95, 118, 222–23
as watershed, 210
See also Poor People's Campaign (1968)
segregation. *See* Jim Crow
Selma campaign (1965), 70–71, 182, 202–3
Service Employees International Union (SEIU), 208
shared experience of poverty, xi, 29–31
Black-only activism myth and, 72
grief and, 224–25
homelessness and, 205–6
hunger for fusion movements and, 35–36
potential power and, xiv
wounds and, 130–31
See also fusion movements; inevitable division myth; white shared interests myth

About the Authors

Reverend Dr. William J. Barber II is Professor in the Practice and Founding Director of the Center for Public Theology and Public Policy at Yale Divinity School. He serves as president and senior lecturer of Repairers of the Breach and cochair of the Poor People's Campaign: A National Call for Moral Revival. A bishop with the Fellowship of Affirming Ministries, he preaches widely and is a regular commentator on cable news shows and the op-ed pages of national newspapers.

Jonathan Wilson-Hartgrove is an assistant director at the Center for Public Theology and Public Policy at Yale Divinity School. He lives with his family at the Rutba House, a house of hospitality in Durham, North Carolina.